WHEN THE NORMANS CAME TO IRELAND

Published in 1998 by
Mercier Press
5 French Church Street Cork
Tel: (021) 275040; Fax (021) 274969
E-mail: books@mercier.ie
16 Hume Street Dublin 2
Tel: (01) 661 5299; Fax: (01) 661 8583
E-mail: books@marino.ie

Trade enquiries to CMD Distribution
55A Spruce Avenue
Stillorgan Industrial Park
Blackrock County Dublin
Tel: (01) 294 2556; Fax: (01) 294 2564

© Maurice Sheehy 1975
ISBN 1 85635 267 6

10 9 8 7 6 5 4 3 2 1

A CIP record for this title is available
from the British Library

Cover design by Liam Furlong
Printed in Ireland by ColourBooks,
Baldoyle Industrial Estate, Dublin 13

WHEN THE NORMANS CAME TO IRELAND

MAURICE SHEEHY

MERCIER PRESS

Publishers' Note

When Maurice Sheehy prepared this book for publication in 1975 he excluded every *síniú fada* (the vowel-lengthening diacritic) from Irish words and names. To preserve the integrity of the original text and to avoid confusion and possible errors, we have maintained that approach in this edition.

CONTENTS

Foreword

This book is not primarily concerned with institutions; political, legal or ecclesiastical. It is concerned with the fact that no constitutional structure or administrative organisation adequately or accurately reflects the mind, ideals or aims of man. It attempts to apply this fact to a period of Irish history when enormous constitutional changes might be said to have taken place.

It is almost a habit with historians to complain of the paucity of their source material in some way or other. I add nothing to the well-nigh universal complaints of others who deal with medieval Irish history. It must be said, however, that literary sources in themselves are not sufficient evidence for the cultural wellsprings of a people, if the findings are not amply supported by evidence from the administrative and legal sources. The evidence for this brief book is selected from every type of source; the danger to avoid in this kind of study is the use of evidence that is merely selective.

The Norman invasion was an event of huge importance in Irish history. Major changes in the structure of society were to follow gradually. Did the constitutional changes bring about equal changes in the minds and hearts of the people, or did the people bend the new shell to their own liking?

M.P.S.

1

THE COMING OF THE NORMANS

Irish sources cursorily note the coming and presence of 'foreigners' during the second half of the twelfth century. In the local Annals, neither the coming nor the presence of these 'foreigners' seems any more ominous than the comings and goings of potential native enemies forty or fifty miles away. Unlike the Norman accounts of the invasion, the native sources show little realisation that the country had been occupied. Nor does the literature of the succeeding period show much sign that something tragic had happened. When certain territories are taken over by the 'grey foreigners' – to distinguish them from the 'black foreigners' or Scandinavians who had settled in some coastal areas since the ninth century – native sources do not regard the area as permanently occupied. This understanding of events reflects the incomplete conquest and balances the accounts given in other sources. The newcomers did not occupy except in the sense that they formed a superficial, but united, ascendancy, and replaced many native Irish rulers. This new ascendancy formed a thin crust at the top, but it had little influence over the Gaelic speaking population, and the newcomers were soon to be absorbed in a way of life that was foreign to their peers in England. The invasion marked a new beginning in centralised government and Dublin was to become the centre of colonial power, but in a society where 'one of the best-founded traditions was that of "white martyrdom", death in exile, which to the poor Irishman meant some outlandish place like Armagh or Lismore', the doings of the 'foreigners' in Dublin were not especially relevant.

The ability to absorb alien elements – the distinguishing feature of that phenomenon known as the hibernisation of the English – played havoc with wave after wave of English colonists. By the time another wave arrived, the previous group was beginning to act and talk like the natives.

Yet from the political point of view, the Norman invasion was an English and papal victory, and it tied the island to the British monarchy for nearly eight centuries. It was the organisational weakness of the Irish mind, and the apparent political chaos, which enabled the better armed invaders to gain a foothold in the first place.[1]

Before the establishment of the Norman kingdom, the inhabitants of England had shown interest in Irish affairs. the foundation of the diocese of Dublin, with the assistance of the bishops of Canterbury, pre-dated the battle of Hastings by a number of decades. After 1066 this interest in the ecclesiastical affairs of Ireland became distinctly predatory.

When the native Irish hierarchy was established by apostolic authority at the synod of Kells in 1152, 'the imperialism of Canterbury had the ground taken out from beneath its feet, but Norman aggression was not thereby checkmated.'² Reaction was swift. Within one or two years a project was worked up in influential circles to replace Anglo-Norman ecclesiastical dominance with an all-out military assault. The sources tell us plainly that it was the English bishops and clergy (*episcopi et religiosi viri*) who promoted the invasion project. An army had been prepared under the leadership of the king's brother. A meeting to discuss it was held at Winchester on 29 September 1155. It was here that King Henry II rejected the idea, pleading the opposition of the Empress Matilda, his mother.³

The meeting at Winchester did not bring an end to intrigue during the pontificate of Hadrian IV – the only Englishman ever to become Pope. Sometime in the following ten months, the confidant and personal envoy of Archbishop Theobold of Canterbury, John of Salisbury, obtained from Hadrian full papal approval for the invasion plan. John of Salisbury, who died as bishop of Chartres in 1178, was the friend of St Bernard of Clairvaux, of Archbishop Theobold and of Thomas Becket. It was as Nicholas Breakspeare, abbot of St Albans, that John had first met the future Hadrian IV, and a bond of friendship had developed between them. Sometime between November 1155 and July 1156 John spent three months with the Pope at Beneventum, and it was during this visit that he obtained papal approval for the English invasion of Ireland. He describes the event himself:

It was at my request that he (the Pope) granted to the illustrious king of England, Henry, the heredi-tary possession of Ireland, as his letters, still extant, attest: for all islands are reputed to belong by long-established right to the Church at Rome, to which they were granted by Constantine, who established and endowed it. Moreover by me he sent the king a golden ring, adorned with a fine emerald, in token of his investiture with the government of Ireland; and this ring is still, by the king's command, preserved in the public treasury.'[4]

John of Salisbury did not transcribe the text of the document which he obtained from the Pope. Giraldus Cambrensis copied a document which he claims is the text of the bull granted by Hadrian IV at John's request. The difficulty about this claim is that the text transcribed by Giraldus can hardly be said to be the text described by John of Salisbury. Archbishop Theobald's envoy was not a canonist, but no man of John of Salisbury's training, experience and learning could unwittingly describe *Laudabiliter et satis*, the bull copied by Giraldus, in terms of a grant of Ireland to Henry II as an hereditary fief. Nor is there mention of the ring or of investiture in Giraldus' text. This has been a real difficulty. It is a problem 'which provides us with the unending amusement of controverting the authenticity of the bull *Laudabiliter*.'[5]

Is it possible to gainsay the report of John of Salisbury? Can it be doubted that Pope Hadrian IV did make a feudal grant of Ireland to King Henry II of England? No English king claimed to be king of Ireland until Henry VIII, in different circumstances, had his parliament raise him to this office. If John of Salisbury's report is accurate, the bull he obtained was never used and it seems to have vanished almost as soon as it was issued. On the other hand, if *Laudabiliter et satis* is the text he was referring to, then he is guilty of exaggeration at least, and probably deliberate falsification.[6] In this case, Hadrian IV did not give a new hereditary fief to Henry II – he simply advocated a crusade.

Laudabiliter et satis, the text transcribed by Giraldus, bears all the marks of authenticity and genuineness; there is nothing to indicate that it was forged. Not alone does it appear to be a genuine papal document, but it bears the signs of having been composed by the curial writers of Hadrian IV's administration.[7]

The content of Hadrian's bull has always been an affront to the Irish people. According to his letter, Hadrian, like his fellow-countrymen, was prepared to look upon the projected military invasion in the light of a crusade or holy war against a degenerate and wayward people.

LAUDABILITER

Hadrian, bishop, servant of the servants of God, to the most beloved son in Christ, the illustrious king of the English, greetings and apostolic blessing.

It is praiseworthy and indeed fruitful for your highness to think of spreading the glorious name of God on earth and to lay up for yourself the reward of eternal happiness in heaven, by proposing – as becomes a catholic prince – to enlarge the boundaries of the Church, to proclaim the truth of the Christian faith to unsophisticated and unlearned peoples, and to root out the weeds of vice from the field of the Lord; and to carry this out more suitably

13

you seek the advice and favour of the Apostolic See. In such a project, the nobler your intention and the greater your caution, the more satisfactory, we trust with God's help, will be your progress: for whatever springs from zeal for the faith and love of religion always leads to good results and a fortunate conclusion. For, as your excellency acknowledges, there is no doubt that Ireland and all the islands upon which Christ, the sun of righteousness, has shone and which have accepted the lessons of the Christian faith, are subject to the law of St Peter and of the holy Roman Church. Consequently we are more concerned to sow in them seed acceptable to God and to plant a nursery faithful to Him, because, as our conscience tells us, we foresee that for them a more strict account will be demanded of us. Since then, most beloved son in Christ, you have notified us that you wish to go into the island of Ireland for the purpose of subjecting that people to the laws and to root out the weeds of vice, and that you are willing to pay an annual pension of one *denarius* from each house, and that you are prepared to preserve the rights of the churches of that land whole and entire, we therefore, likewise endorsing with fitting approval your pious and praiseworthy desire and extending a willing assent to your petition, welcome and accept that you should march into that island and carry out whatever tends to the honour of God and the welfare of that land, and that your purpose shall be to enlarge the boundaries of the Church, to restrain the downward course of vice, to correct evil habits and introduce virtue and to increase the Christian religion: and we also agree that the people of that land shall receive you honourably and respect you as their Lord, as long as the rights of the churches are permanently preserved whole and entire as well as the annual pension of one *denarius* from each house to St Peter and the holy Roman Church. If therefore, you are led to carry out what you have proposed, be careful to teach good habits to the people, and act, both personally and through any agents who appear in belief, word and life, to be suitable, in such a way that the Church there will be adorned and that the religion of Christian faith be sown and grow: let your ruling be whatever tends to the honour of God and to the salvation of souls, so that you may merit mercy from the everlasting God and obtain on earth a glorious name forever.'[8]

All the attempts to prove *Laudabiliter* a forgery by discrediting Giraldus Cambrensis' integrity as a witness have been lost efforts. There is no good reason for doubting the genuineness of Habrian IV's letter of approval. It was simply the first in a long series of papal documents which endorsed the Norman crusade, and which introduced a new pressure into Irish affairs. On the whole, it was a pressure which the English and Anglo-Irish were adept at manipulating for their own ends, but even at the lowest ebb of its involvement with politics and economics, the papacy never entirely abandoned its primary spiritual mission. There were times when the papal authority could be turned in matters of justice and equity by Irish and Anglo-Irish churchmen against the English powers. But for the major portion of the *ecclesia inter Hibernos* much of the authority claimed by the papacy was not understood and was ignored as irrelevant.

It was not difficult to couch the idea of the invasion in terms of a crusade to strengthen the Christian religion since most of the interested parties in the twelfth century, some Irish as well as outsiders, presented a gloomy picture of the state of religion. But John of Salisbury also used convincing political arguments to gain the favour of the Pope. Hadrian himself had introduced the idea of Peter's Pence while legate in Scandinavia, and the notion of the papal rights over islands appears both in John of Salisbury's *Metalogicon* and in *Laudabiliter*.

Despite John of Salisbury's successful mission to the Pope, there was no immediate attempt to put the crusade into effect. Henry II had other things on his mind. Nevertheless the ground was now well laid, and when the first Norman barons did come more than a decade later on the invitation of an Irish provincial king, Henry II had no qualms in coming after them. The papacy was involved in the Norman invasion from the beginning.

THE INVASION

The very incoherence of Irish society, which made it difficult to consolidate any military conquest, was also the immediate reason for the success of the invasion. Almost continuous battle had been done for centuries among the loosely organised tribal kingdoms for provincial hegemony, and since the tenth century, for countrywide overlordship. After a long struggle between O Briain of Munster, O Conchubhair of Connacht and Mac Lochlainn from the north, the high-kingship of Ireland was won in 1161 by Muirchertach Mac Lochlainn. This victory for his ally suited Diarmuid Mac Murchadha, king of Leinster, admirably. But the death of Mac Lochlainn in 1166 – an event of enormous significance in Irish political history – brought an end to the northern hegemony and left the way open for the rise to the high-kingship of Ruaidhri O Conchubhair, king of Connacht. This turn of events was disastrous for the king of Leinster, for not only was he on the worst of terms with the O Conchubhair family, but his most bitter enemy was Tighernan O Ruairc, the ruler of Breifni, whose aid had enabled Ruaidhri O Conchubhair to gain supremacy. When O Ruairc advanced into Leinster late in 1166, Diarmuid Mac Murchadha fled the country. In the following year he returned to Ireland with a small levy of Normans, Flemings and Welshmen and earned for himself the epithet *Diarmuid na nGall*. Although Diarmuid, with the help of his foreign mercenaries, re-established himself in his old territory of Ui Chenselaigh, little attention was paid to this minor victory. But when he renewed his claim to his lost title, king of Leinster, the high-king moved against him. Mac Murchadha was defeated but in the agreement which followed he was allowed to retain Ui Chenselaigh on condition that he recognised Ruaidhri O Conchubhair's supremacy and abandoned his plans for the recovery of the eastern province. Tighernan O Ruairc used the occasion to extract an indemnity for the personal injury he had suffered through Diarmuid Mac Murchadha's eloping with his wife, Dervorgilla. But the wily Mac Murchadha was only biding his time and on 1 May 1169 further reinforcements under Maurice Prendergast, Hervey de Montmorency and Robert FitzStephen came from Wales and landed at Bannow Bay on the south Wexford coast. Diarmuid once more took the field but again he was defeated by Ruaidhri O Conchubhair. An attempt to establish peace, inspired by Archbishop Laurence O'Toole of Dublin, resulted in negotiations which led to the treaty of 1169. Diarmuid was recognised as king of Leinster on the understanding that he would recognise Ruaidhri as high-king: he also undertook, in a secret clause, to send his foreign allies back whence they came.

Diarmuid Mac Murchadha was no more to be trusted in 1169 than in 1167. He now wrote to Richard Fitz-Gilbert de Clare (Strongbow), earl of Pembroke and Striguil, urging him to redeem his promise of aid made during the original negotiations for Norman help in 1167. To Earl Richard he held out 'not only the prospect of succession to the kingdom of Leinster as the future husband of his daughter Aoifa, but also the prospect of the succession to the high-kingship of Ireland, though both these prospects involved violation of the Irish Laws of succession.' With the cautious permission (later revoked) of King Henry II, Richard de Clare determined to take his chance. He sent over Maurice FitzGerald and Raymond Carew and prepared to follow himself. He arrived in Ireland with a strong force on 23 August 1170. By 25 August he had taken the town of Waterford which had risen against Diarmuid. A few days later he was married to Aoifa, the daughter of the king of Leinster, in the cathedral of the town. 'By this marriage Strongbow became heir-in-succession to Leinster at such time as Diarmuid should die. It was sound enough in feudal law; but in Irish law it was unknown that a man should acquire a kingdom by right of a woman, whether mother or wife. Diarmuid was setting aside the elective right of his royal stock and depriving his sons and his brothers of their right to succeed him. But victory in the field was the immediate need, and both sides realised the importance of Dublin.'[9]

The people of Dublin, like those in Waterford, had revolted against Diarmuid Mac Murchadha when the second wave of Normans came in 1170. The local ruler and ally of the high-king, Asgall Mac Torcaill, now arranged to join forces with Ruaidhri O Conchubhair in defence of the town. But Diarmuid and Earl Richard got there first; before the citizens had time to make contact with the king of Ireland's army, the allied enemy appeared unexpectedly before the gates. Negotiations were opened under the aegis of Archbishop Laurence, but since both he and the Dubliners refused to break faith with the high-king, the town was suddenly taken by storm and burned while Asgall Mac Torcaill fled for help. Dublin was taken on 21 September 1170. Before the end of the year most of Leinster had been reduced by the Norman-Irish army and forays carried into Meath and the south. But 'the great prize of victory was Dublin'[10] and before leaving it Diarmuid and Earl Richard appointed Miles de Cogan as its constable. Richard de Clare retired to Waterford and Diarmuid Mac Murchadha to his winter quarters in Leinster.

Meanwhile the high-king, who had kept his army intact, intervened to remind Mac Murchadha of the treaty of 1169 and to bid him dismiss his foreign allies. Diarmuid's answer was to outline the full ambitions of his programme 'which was nothing less than the defeat of the Irish armies, the overthrow of the existing government and the winning of the high-kingship for himself (and presumably also for his Anglo-Norman heir)'.[11] Diarmuid Mac Murchadha was not to see any of his ambitions realised; he died at the beginning of the following May, 1171 at Ferns and left 'Strongbow king of Leinster and heir to the programme of a complete conquest of Ireland'.[12]

Their successes in the autumn of 1170, and the capture of Dublin suddenly made the arrival of the Normans a matter of general concern. For the hierarchy, the only nationwide organisation, it should be a portentous challenge. Archbishop Laurence of Dublin was already deeply involved; his efforts to hold off the Norman party before Dublin had failed. In the north, Archbishop Gille Mhic Liag of Armagh was a feeble man of over 80 years. Nevertheless it was decided that a meeting of the bishops should be held to deal with the question. Thus Laurence, with as many bishops as he could muster, journeyed north where a synod was convened at Armagh. We know of only one of their resolutions; it was a decree very relevant to the political situation. Giraldus records his version of it. Since for a long time the Irish had been wont 'to purchase natives of England from traders, robbers and pirates and to reduce them to slavery, wherefore they were now themselves by reciprocal justice reduced to slavery by that very same nation . . . the synod decreed that all Englishmen throughout Ireland who were in a state of bondage should be restored to freedom.'[13]

Shortly after the death of Diarmuid Mac Murchadha the Irish offensive began again. Dublin, now more than ever, was the key to victory. But the first attack on the town by Asgal Mac Torcaill failed and the ruler of Dublin was himself captured and executed. Thereafter followed a long seige of the city by a confederate army under O Conchubhair, the high-king, O Ruairc of Breifne and O Cearbhaill of Oirghialla. The town was blockaded for two months. Richard de Clare was forced to negotiate. He requested Archbishop Laurence to convey an offer of terms to the high-king. 'The earl now offered to recognise the high-kingship of O Conchubhair and to do homage for the kingdom of Leinster. This amounted to an offer to return to the principles of the treaty of 1169 on the invader's side, if the native authorities would agree to accept the Norman leader as the heir and successor of Mac Murchadha.'[14] But the high-king saw no reason why Richard de Clare would be more likely to observe the treaty of 1169 once his present difficulties were overcome, than Diarmuid Mac Murchadha had been. He therefore refused the offer and made a counter-offer which would limit de Clare's authority in Ireland to the towns of Dublin, Wexford and Waterford. These terms were unacceptable to the Normans and both sides prepared for further battle.

As it happened the besieged had a much easier victory than they might have expected. A sortie out of the town at an auspicious moment routed a larger but carelessly organised Irish army. A 'multitude' of the Irish were slain and sufficient provisions for a whole year were captured. So ended the last united military stand in face of this foreigner. A later attack on Dublin by O Ruairc during the absence of Richard de Clare was easily repulsed by the town garrison under Miles de Cogan.

What is of particular interest at this stage is the watchful eye which Henry of Anjou had been keeping on even the most remotely placed Norman barons. Their success in Ireland in 1170 gave the Angevin king little cause for complacency; the succession of Richard Fitz-Gilbert de Clare, earl of Pembroke, to the kingdom of Leinster in May 1171 spurred him into action. Determined that a new Norman kingdom should not arise beyond the western sea Henry II obtained the approval of a council at Argentan in July for his coming to Ireland. His immediate purpose in coming was clearly evident before he landed. On the way he was met by a submissive Earl Richard at Newham in Gloucestershire. The king's anger at the earl's independent ways was not appeased until de Clare offered him his Irish gains. Henry II landed at Waterford on 17 October 1171 with a large army, and immediately set about consolidating for the English monarchy the conquests which his barons had made. To Richard de Clare he granted the land of Leinster as a fief, but the towns of Dublin, Waterford and Wexford, as well as the kingdom of Dublin, he reserved to the crown. He reached Dublin on 11 November 1171 and made it for the first time the official capital of the country. Hugh de Lacy was appointed governor of the town and viceroy of Ireland. Except for Ruaidhri O Conchubhair the high-

22

king and a handful of northern and western leaders, most of the Irish rulers submitted to, or as the Irish themselves understood it, 'came into the house of', the Angevin king of England. Thus, through the adventures of his fellow Norman barons whom he had followed to control, Henry II, almost involuntarily and certainly without a battle, became ruler of the land which he had refused to invade a decade and a half before.

There was another immediate advantage in the Irish situation for Henry II. Recently (20 December 1170) he had overstrained the relations between the English monarchy and the spiritual powers by the murder of Archbishop Thomas Becket of Canterbury. A peace offering unconnected with the local English dispute would help heal the breach in relations with the papacy. Pope Alexander III's predecessor had already encouraged a holy war from England against the barbarous Irish. The Norman invasion might be presented in the light of this very crusade so piously desired by the Popes.

Having received recognisances from a number of the Irish kings and princes – who clearly intended to recognise Henry II's overlordship in the sense of Irish law and not to make the feudal submission which the English king had in mind – Henry II arranged with the resident papal legate, Bishop Christian O Conairce of Lismore, to hold a council of the bishops of Ireland. The council was to be concerned with the continuation of the twelfth-century Irish reform movement, and it was a great victory for Henry II that so many representatives attended. As well as the papal legate, the three archbishops of Cashel, Dublin and Tuam were present and some 28 other bishops from the four metropolitan provinces. On the other hand, also present were Ralph the archdeacon of Llandaff, Nicholas the royal chaplain and other clerics and ambassadors of the king of England. The royal representatives, if they did not run the affair, played a vital role in the direction of the proceedings.

Giraldus' version of the last decree of the Council of Cashel is followed by his own significant comment: 'Since proper reverence in the obsequies should be rendered to those who die after a good confession, both in the celebrating of Masses and holding of vigils and in the manner of burial, so all divine services are to be carried out in all parts of the Church in Ireland . . . according to what the English Church observes. For it is right and just that, as by divine providence Ireland received her lord and king from England, she should also submit to a reformation from the same source.'[15]

Two things happened at the Council of Cashel. The Irish bishops were induced to sign a report on the religious state of the country. This was a distinctly unsavoury and harsh report, which had been drawn up mainly by the king's representatives. In the second place, reform legislation was passed based on this report. But the report was further used by Henry II to accompany his own letters to the Pope, and to present an acceptable view of the Norman invasion. It was the king's principal ambassador, Ralph the archdeacon of Llandaff, who brought these documents to the curia, and who – as the Pope notes in his reply – suitably embellished the episcopal report from Ireland. Conveniently, no mention was made of the reform decrees, or even that the Council of Cashel, as a reform measure, had been held. The Pope's information then, was that religious conditions in Ireland were in a critical state – and on this point he had before him the report of the Irish bishops themselves. Secondly, it appeared that the good king Henry was the only hope for an improvement in Christian affairs. The appearances are that the bishops, still trying to establish their dioceses, had placed great hopes in the English king. The tone of the letters of Alexander III suggests that the hierarchy was hopelessly dependent on Henry II.

For the Popes at this time, the land of Ireland was merely 'the kingdom which the Roman emperors, conquerors of the world had left untouched.' And the suggestion is that it had been too backward and corrupt for the emperors to bother. Hadrian IV and Alexander III admitted that Christianity had been preached and adopted there, but clearly Irish Christianity was a puny thing in comparison with the *Christianitas* of the European tradition.

Three letters, dated 20 September 1172, were brought back from Tusculum by the king's agent. The constitutional thinking behind these documents, not to mention the sycophantic references to the murderer of Archbishop Becket, presents a mind hardly comprehensible to the native Irishman.[16]

Alexander, bishop, servant of the servants of God to the venerable brothers Christian bishop of Lismore and legate of the Apostolic See, and Gille, Domhnall, Laurence and Cadhla archbishops of Armagh, Cashel, Dublin and Tuam, and to their suffragans, greetings and apostolic blessing.

It has been made known to us from a series of your letters, as it has equally come often to the notice of the Apostolic See by the truthful account of others, that the Irish race has been infected by so many enormities of vice, and how, having cast aside the religion of the Christian faith and the fear of God, it pursues that which incurs risk of souls. Hence assuredly, we are overjoyed – discovering from your letters that by the might of our most dear son in Christ, Henry the illustrious king of the English, who, stirred by divine inspirations, with his united forces, subjected that barbarous, un-cultured race, ignorant of the divine law, to his authority, and that those things which were illicitly practised in your land have already, with the help of the Lord, begun to stop and we have offered great thanks to Him who has brought such a victory and triumph to the aforesaid king. By humble prayers we have asked that, through the vigilance and solicitude of that king, and with your careful cooperation, that unruly and unconquered race may follow the worship of divine law and the religion of the Christian faith always and in all things, and that you and the other ecclesiastics may enjoy honour and a deserved peace. Therefore, because it is proper that you should apply diligent care and goodwill to furthering those things, still unfinished, which have had such a holy beginning, we enjoin and instruct you by apostolic letters, diligently and firmly in so far as your order and office allows you, to assist that king as a great man and most devoted son of the Church, to know and maintain that land and to root out from it the filth of such abominations. And if any of the kings, princes or other men of that land shall rashly attempt to flout what he owes by oath and by fealty shown to the king, and if after your warning he does not quickly come to his senses as he should, you shall, disregarding all excuses and delays, strike him with ecclesiastical censure with the full support of the Apostolic See. So carry out our command diligently and effectively, just as the aforesaid king as a catholic and most Christian ruler is said to have listened favourably and kindly to your request to have both titles and other ecclesiastical rights and all things which refer to ecclesiastical liberty restored, in the same way you stoutly defend everything which touches the royal dignity and, as far as you can, have them preserved by others.

Alexander bishop ... to the most beloved son in Christ, Henry, the illustrious king of the English ...

Gladly and with great satisfaction we have learned by notorious accounts and by reliable reports from many people that, as befits a devout king and great leader, you have – with the help of the Lord as we devoutly believe – marvellously extended your power over the ignorant and undisciplined Irish people, who, rejecting the fear of God, stubbornly and unrestrainedly wallow in vice and reject the practice of virtue and of the Christian faith and spend their time slaughtering one another, and that you have magnificently triumphed over that kingdom which, we understand, the Roman emperors, conquerors of the world, left untouched in their time. For, passing over for the present the other wickedness and vice to which that people are enslaved, irreverently heedless of the practice of the Christian faith – as our venerable brothers Christian bishop of Lismore and legate of the Apostolic See and the archbishops and bishops of that land have made known to us in their letters, and as Ralph the archdeacon of Llandaf, a wise and prudent man and one especially devoted to your royal Highness (who has seen these things with his own eyes), has verbally and with care and detail related to us, that people – as perhaps your serene Majesty is more fully aware – openly marry their stepmothers and unashamedly beget children by them; a man will take advantage of his brother's wife while the brother is still alive; a man will live in concubinage with two sisters; and many of them, abandoning their wives, marry their [step-] daughters; and throughout Lent all eat meat, they pay no tithes, and have no reverence whatsoever for the sacred churches of God or for ecclesiastical persons, as they should. As we learn from these archbishops and bishops and more fully and explicitly from the aforesaid archdeacon's report to us, you, inspired by divine mercy, have gathered together your powerful naval and land forces and have bestirred yourself to subject that people to your lordship and to root out such filthy abominations, and this we wholeheartedly welcome – as indeed we ought – and devoutly give thanks for this to Him from Whom all good comes and Who accounts for the pious acts and intentions of His faithful towards their salvation. We beseech the Lord almighty with prayers of intercession that as those illicit things done in the aforementioned country are beginning to decrease and instead of vice the shoots of virtue are spreading through the power of your Majesty, so with the help of the Lord the said people may, through you, embrace the full practice of the Christian faith and cast aside the filth of their sins, and thus bring you an imperishable crown of eternal glory and to themselves bring salvation. We therefore ask, enjoin and exhort your royal Highness in the Lord, and lay upon you for the remission of your sins, that you should the more readily strengthen and fortify your intention in what you have so praiseworthily begun and call back that people to Christian worship by your power and keep them in it, so that as you have undertaken such a task among them for the forgiveness of your sins, as we believe, so also you may deserve to obtain an eternal crown by bringing about their salvation. And because, as your most excellent Majesty knows, the Roman Church has different rights in islands than over continents, and since we are hopeful and confident of your fervent devotion that you wish not only to preserve the rights of the Church but also to add to them and where it has no right that you ought to establish them, we ask and anxiously warn your Majesty that you should take pains to preserve for Us the rights of St Peter in the abovementioned land and that, if there are none there, by your greatness you will establish and assign those rights to that Church, thereby obliging Us to render great thanks to your royal Highness and showing that you have offered to God the first fruits of your glory and triumph.

Alexander . . . to the beloved sons, noblemen, kings and princes of Ireland . . .

Since it has come to our notice by common report and the reliable account of many people that you have accepted our most dear son in Christ, Henry, illustrious king of England, as your king and lord, and have sworn fealty to him we are all the more overjoyed because by the power of the same king there will be greater peace and quiet in your land with the Lord's help, and the Irish race which has seemed to have gone so far astray through monstrous and filthy vice will now the more willingly be turned towards divine worship and will all the better practice the Christian faith. So we praise and endorse, as is fitting, your far-sightedness in submitting yourselves freely and willingly to such a powerful and great king and so devoted a son of the Church, because thence great profit can be expected to come to yourselves, to the Church and to all the people of that land. We anxiously warn your lordships and enjoin upon you that you take care to preserve unwavering and inviolate the fealty which you have sworn on the gospel to so great a king, with appropriate submission, and thus show yourselves humbly and meekly obedient and devoted to him, so that you may always have his abundant favour and we may thereby be obliged to commend your wisdom.

That the information reaching the Pope was concerned with the Norman invasion and its justification – and not with the reform Council of Cashel – is clear from the papal reply. Unlike Pope Urban III's answer to the reports from the provincial Council of Dublin in 1186, not only is the legislation not endorsed in detail by Alexander III, but the fact of the council is never mentioned. The invasion had been successfully presented as a crusade to a thoroughly degenerate people. That mention had been made of Hadrian IV's letter in support of the invasion project is probable – Alexander refers to the king's obedience to the papal wishes in establishing ecclesiastical rights and liberties, and to the doctrine of papal rights over islands. That Henry II used this crusade to gain papal pardon and goodwill is suggested by Alexander's letter to Henry – 'even as you have for the remission of your sins undertaken so great a task.'

From his point of view, the visit of Henry II to Ireland was a huge success. He had established effective royal control over his liegemen in a new territory, he had successfully obtained papal approval for the venture and made sure of papal pardon for his earlier misdemeanour, and he had, insofar as his intentions for the future were concerned, largely fooled the natives into accepting him as their lord.

From the contemporary Irish point of view, on the other hand, the Norman invasion was altogether a different event. It was not seen as a further stage in Norman expansion, nor as an extension of centralised ecclesiastical government. Indeed it was not seen as a permanent development until time forced this conclusion on the more reflective. And even then, the explanations of the change have a practical, narrow and concrete stamp. In the late thirteenth century, one commentator declared in a note: 'Ua Ardocc and Ua Cellchin of Cell More, Ua Sluaisti of Cuil O Sluaisti, Ua Glesain, they it was who stole horses and mules and asses of the cardinal [Vivian] who came from Rome to Ireland [1175] to instruct them in the time of Domnall Mor O Briain, king of Munster [1168-1194]. That is why the successor (*comarba*) of Peter sold the tax and tribute of Ireland to the Saxons. And this is the right and claim that the Saxons follow today upon the Gaels. For until then the tax and tribute of Ireland used to go to the *comarba* of Peter in Rome.'[17]

There is, of course, a lot of substance behind the contemporary Irish attitude. For them, in many ways perhaps, the tragedy was that the English king never became their ruler. The pattern was set by Henry II. For the future the English monarchy merely kept loose reins on the colonists in Ireland.

The spectacle that presented itself to Norman eyes when they arrived in Ireland in the second half of the twelfth century must have seemed bizarre at least. Giraldus makes no secret of the fact that it was like coming into another world. Notwithstanding his Welsh background he was clearly baffled when he came over with the early invaders. Although he travelled widely and was in close touch with both local churchmen and the Norman authorities, his account of the state of Ireland in the *Topographia Hibernica* is full of contradictory impressions and annoyance at the intangible complexities.

On a number of points the account of Giraldus Cambrensis serves to confirm the complaints of earlier outside observers. The Christian marriage code was widely ignored – the complaints on this score go back through Pope Alexander III and Bernard of Clairvaux to the first council of Cashel in 1101, and Lanfranc. The same is true of certain rites and ceremonies inherited from a pre-Christian age, and of tithes. On other points Giraldus shows some progress in outside understanding and unlike Bernard of Clairvaux he does not confuse the hereditary ecclesiastical families with the men in episcopal orders. Although he obviously does not understand how the clergy fit into society, nonetheless he is able to discern an amount of virtue in their lives. Compared with Giraldus' world – the world of the ecclesiastical politician angling for office from the hands of his liege lord – the apparent lack of pastoral concern in Ireland merits the full wrath of his condemnation. And although he did notice that the notion of liberty and individual freedom seemed to be an extremely important factor in Irish life, he failed to see that this notion might be equally applicable in matters of faith – and that his idea of pastoral concern might be entirely irrelevant in this different world.

Giraldus does a service when he highlights the fact

that Irish life developed out of very different roots and that its isolation had caused it to grow away from the mainstream of medieval Europe. The Irish mind was now a distinct phenomenon – baffling and intangible to the outsider, in itself deeply mistrustful of the better organised and more materially powerful alien world. Under the full impact of foreign occupation it remained a distinct discernible phenomenon, absorbing wave after wave of colonists and engulfing them. This was to cause two worlds in post-invasion Ireland and two Christian Churches.

The *Topographia Hibernica* of Giraldus Cambrensis was written for and addressed to the English king. The author's expectations of ecclesiastical preferment depended on Henry II and one must therefore expect that his description of Ireland will be calculated to endorse and confirm the view which the king so carefully presented to the Pope. Allowing for the bias of one of the king's men and for the author's admitted inability to fully understand this alien environment, the tracts of Giraldus are an invaluable insight into how the Anglo-Irish for centuries would regard the Irish. The following extracts are taken from the *Topographia*.[18]

Although the Irish are fully endowed with natural gifts, their external characteristics of beard and dress, and internal cultivation of the mind, are so barbarous that they cannot be said to have any culture. They use very little wool in their dress and that itself nearly always black (because the sheep of that country are black), and made up in a barbarous fashion. For they wear little hoods, close-fitting and stretched across the shoulders and down about a cubit's length, and generally sewn together from cloths of various kinds. Under these they wear mantles instead of cloaks. They also use woollen trousers that are at the same time boots, or boots that are at the same time trousers, and these are for the most part dyed. When riding they do not use saddles, leggings or spurs. They drive on and guide their horses by means of a stick with a crook at its upper end, which they hold in their hand. They regard weapons as a burden and they think it brave and honourable to fight unarmed. They use however three types of weapon – short spears, two darts (in this they imitate the Basques – whence the Irish came), and big axes well and carefully forged, which they have taken over from the Norwegians and the Ostmen. When everything else fails, they are quicker and more expert than any other people in flinging stones as missiles, and such stones do great damage to an enemy in an engagement.

They are a wild and inhospitable people . . . They have not progressed at all from the primitive habits of pastoral living . . . This people depises agriculture, has little use for the money-making of towns, condemns the rights and privileges of citizenship, and desires neither to abandon nor lose respect for the life which it has been accustomed to lead in the woods and countryside. They use fields generally as pasture . . . little is cultivated. The fields are naturally fertile and productive. The nature of the soil is not to be blamed but rather the want of industry on the part of the cultivator. He is too lazy to plant the foreign types of trees that would grow well here. The different types of mineral too . . . are not mined or put to any use, precisely because of the same laziness. They do not devote their lives to the processing of flax or wool, or to any kind of merchandise or mechanical art. For given only to leisure and devoted only to laziness, they think that the greatest wealth is to enjoy liberty.

Judged according to modern ideas these people are uncultivated. They are so removed in these distant parts from the ordinary world of men, as if they were in another world altogether . . . that they know only of the barbarous habits in which they were born and brought up. Their natural qualities are excellent. But almost everything acquired is deplorable.

It is only in the case of musical instruments that I find any commendable diligence in this people. They seem to me to be incomparably more skilled in these than any other people that I have seen . . . Ireland uses and delights in two instruments only, the harp and the timpanum. Scotland uses three, the harp, timpanum and the crowd. Wales uses the harp, the pipes and the crowd.

Although since the time of Patrick and through so many years the Faith has been founded in the island, and has almost continuously thrived, it is nevertheless remarkable that this people even still remains so uninstructed in its rudiments . . . They do no yet pay tithes or first fruits or contract marriages. They do not avoid incest. They do not come to church with due reverence. Moreover . . . men in many places in Ireland, I shall not say marry, but rather debauch, the wives of their dead brothers. They abuse them in having such evil and incestuous relations with them. In this they follow the external teaching, and not the true doctrine, of the Old Testament.

Moreover, above all other people they always practise treachery. When they give their word to anyone, they do not keep it. They do not blush or fear to violate every day the bond of their pledge and oath given to others – although they are very keen that it should be observed with regard to themselves. When you have employed every safe-guard – for your safety and security, both by means of oaths and hostages, and friendships firmly cemented, and all kinds of benefits conferred, then you must be especially on your guard, because then especially their malice seeks a chance.

It must be observed also, that the men who enjoy ecclesiastical immunity, and are called ecclesiastical men, although they be laics, and have wives, and wear long hair handing down below their shoulders, but only do not bear arms, wear for their protection, by authority of the Pope, fillets on the crown of their heads as a mark of distinction. Moreover these people, who have customs so very different from others, and so opposite to them, on making signs either with the hands or the head, beckon when they mean that you should go away, and nod backwards as often as they wish to be rid of you.

The clergy of this country are on the whole to be commended for their observance. Among their other virtues chastity shines out as a kind of special prerogative. They diligently carry out their obligations in the matter of the Psalms and the hours, reading and praying . . . they practise a considerable amount of abstinence and ascetiscism in the use of food . . . I have almost only one thing on which to reprove the bishops and prelates, and that is that they are too slack and negligent in the correction of a people that is guilty of such enormities. If the prelates . . . over the years had done a man's job . . . in preaching and instructing, chastising and correcting, they would have extirpated, at any rate to a certain extent, those abominations of the people already mentioned, and would have impressed upon them some semblance of honour and religious feeling . . . Since nearly all the prelates of Ireland were taken from monasteries into the ranks of the clergy, they scrupulously fulfil all the obligations of a monk. But they omit almost everything to which they are obliged as clerics and prelates.

There are however some among the clergy who are most excellent men, and have no leaven of impunity. Indeed this people are intemperate in all their actions, and most vehement in their feelings. Thus the bad are bad indeed – there are nowhere worse; and than the good you cannot find better.

Giraldus was willing to tell a story against himself. One conversation he had with an Irish archbishop produced from the prelate a prophetic retort. He had been complaining about the lack of knowledge of even the rudiments of the Christian faith among a large section of the people and about the many abuses which he had noticed.

When once I was making these complaints and others like them to Matthew O hEnni the archbishop of Cashel (1185-1206), a learned and discreet man, . . . and was blaming the prelates especially for the terrible enormities of the country, using the very strong argument that no one in that kingdom had ever won the crown of martyrdom in defence of the Church of God, the archbishop gave a reply which cleverly got home − although it did not rebut my point. 'It is true,' he said, 'that our people are very backward, uncivilised and savage. Nevertheless they have always paid great honour and reverence to churchmen and they have never put out their hands against the saints of God. But now a people has come to the kingdom which knows how, and is accustomed to, make martyrs. From now on Ireland will have its martyrs, just as other countries.'

2

THE NORMAN COLONY

The newcomers were relatively few in number, and although in virtue of their superior military prowess they had spread over a great part of the country by the middle of the thirteenth century, they formed but a thin veneer over Irish society. Unlike the earlier Norman conquests in Europe, their penetration in Ireland was only surface deep. For the most part the French-speaking Normans became the overlords of the Irish kings and chieftains, and the traditions of the latter were further perpetuated through Norman intermarriage with the native aristocracy.

Much of our modern political and social organisations owes its origin to the administration and practices introduced by the Normans, the division into counties and liberties, the centralisation of administration and its location in Dublin, the introduction of a special juridical concept of towns and boroughs with its attendant economic and social changes, the establishment of a centralised system of justice with its local and royal courts, the widespread introduction of coinage. But the resultant social and political advantages for the people were a long time in coming. From the beginning, the Irish were excluded from the benefits of English law. And since the 'mere Irish' – to distinguish them from the few recognised Irish chiefts – formed by far the majority, one could attach too much importance to the evolution of English administrative customs in the country. They were applicable only to the minority albeit the ascendancy.[1]

From the very beginning the new sovereign of Ireland, the English king, failed to come to terms with the people in the new dominion. The administrative documents bear out the struggling attempts of the chroniclers to interpret and understand the situation. To outside observers the treacherous sensitivity, the insidiously paralysing inertia and the mercurial elusiveness of the native people left only two alternatives for the colonists; either be swallowed up by this narrow swirling isolated world or keep the Irish at arm's length. The government, perhaps wisely, never seriously deflected from the latter course. Indeed, even in the Anglo-Norman period, those royal officials who became too deeply embroiled in Irish affairs usually ended up at odds with both worlds. Of the newcomers who settled, many were thoroughly absorbed and became barely distinguishable from the natives. Nevertheless, the result was that even though the link with England remained, Ireland was not ruled by the English government. Except where vital imperial interests were concerned, the stalemate between Irish and Anglo-Irish in Ireland was studiously ignored.[2]

Henry II left Ireland on 17 April 1172. Before leaving he confirmed Earl Richard in the kingdom of Leinster and established Hugh de Lacy in the 'earldom of Meath' as a counterweight. He reserved the city and kingdom of

Dublin to the crown as well as the towns of Waterford and Wexford. Hugh de Lacy was made first governor of Ireland and guardian of Dublin. Beyond reaffirming his feudal authority over his own and leaving a special representative to supervise his rights, no provision was made to govern the new dominion. Towards the native aristocracy he adopted a purely pragmatic policy. While he accepted the submission of the Irish kings and chieftains, he did not grant them recognition as feudal vassals and he gave them no charters. On the other hand they certainly would not have asked for royal charters. Their notion of 'going into Henry's house' was not at all what a Norman baron would have in mind. For them it was a matter of giving hostages and homage to an overlord who would grant them recognition without interference. While Henry II in one sense seemed to accept this position, recognising them as elective rulers whose prerogatives and property was held in virtue of their office and whose subjects were bound to them by ancient custom, on the other hand he very soon began to expect feudal tribute. There were thus two incompatible legal conditions in force from the very first days of the English king's relations with Ireland; feudalism the explicit condition of Norman tenure and life, and Irish law and custom the implicit condition for the native aristocracy and lower stratum. The two systems were irreconcilable.

There was wholesale fighting and plunder between Norman and Irish after the departure of Henry II. By 1175, both Henry and the high-king Ruaidhri O Conchubhair were ready to come to terms. A treaty was negotiated, largely by Archbishop Laurence O'Toole. The meeting was held at Windsor and the high-king's envoys were Cadhla O Dubhthaigh the archbishop of Connacht, Cantordis the abbot of St Brendan at Clonfert and *magister* Laurence the 'chancellor of the king of Connacht'. There were two versions of what was decided at Windsor. The official Norman version states:

The king of England has granted to Ruaidhri, his liegeman, king of Connacht, as long as he shall faithfully serve him, that he shall be king under him, ready to his service, as his man. And he shall hold his land as fully and as peacefully as he held it before his lord entered Ireland, rendering him tribute. And that he shall have all the rest of the land and its inhabitants under him and shall bring them to account, so that they shall pay their full tribute to the king of England through him, and so that they shall maintain their rights.

And those who are now in possession of their lands and rights shall hold them as long as they remain in the fealty of the king of England, and continue to pay him faithfully and fully his tribute on the other rights which they owe to him, by the hand of the king of Connacht, saving in all things the right and honour of the king of England and of Ruaidhri. And if any of them shall be rebels to the king of England and to Ruaidhri and shall refuse to pay the tribute and other rights of the king of England by his hand, and shall withdraw from the fealty of the king of England, he, Ruaidhri, shall judge them and remove them. And if he cannot answer for them by himself, the constable of the king of England in that land shall, when called upon by him, aid him to do what is necessary. And for this agreement the said king of Connacht shall render to the king of England tribute every year . . . save that he shall not meddle with those lands which the lord king has retained in his lordshp and in the lordship of his barons; that is to say . . .

And if the Irish who have fled wish to return to the land of the barons of the king of England they may do so in peace, paying the said tribute as others pay it, or doing to the English the services *which they were wont to do* for their lands, which shall be decided by the judgment and will of their lords. And if any of them are unwilling to return and their lords have called upon the king of Connacht, he shall compel them to return to their land, so that they shall dwell there in peace.'[3]

The Irish version, on the other hand, rejects the implied partition of the country into two different legal and political systems. According to the Annals:

Cadhla O Dubhthaigh returned from the land of the Saxons, from the son of the empress, having with him the peace of Ireland, and the kingship of Ireland, both Foreigner and Gael, to Ruaidhri O Conchubhair and to every provincial king in his province from the king of Ireland, and their tribes to Ruaidhri.[4]

The two sides were not talking about the same things at all.

The reference in the English version to the return of the Irish who had fled indicates a Norman policy which was distinctly two-edged. On the one hand, by enticing the Irish to return to their holdings, either on feudal or customary Irish terms, the great earls of the early days showed shrewd economic wisdom. By establishing garrisoned castles and manors occupied by their own vassals and fellow-knights at strategic points, their fiefs were protected despite the presence of the Irish. On the other hand, by allowing traditional Irish custom and law to govern their relations with their subjects who farmed the land, the first step was taken in the eventual undermining of their own feudal relations with the outside world. Coupled with intermarriage with the Irish aristocracy, this policy tended further to engulf the newcomers in the Irish system.

The treaty of Windsor did nothing to stabilise the situation. The Earl Richard died in Dublin on 1 June 1176. He was replaced as governor by a small council of barons under William FitzAudelin. One of these, John de Courcy was soon heading north with a band of warriors. The superiority of Norman arms was just as effective in the north as it had been in the east and south. Within a brief space of time de Courcy had carved out a semi-independent kingdom for himself in Ulster. Meantime in May 1177 Henry II held a council of his barons at Oxford to deal with Ireland. Ignoring the treaty of two years previously, large new grants were made of territory in Leinster and Munster, to Norman barons and knights.

The McCarthy kingdom went to Milo de Cogan and Robert FitzStephen, and the O Briain kingdom to Philip de Braose. The towns of Cork and Limerick were reserved to the crown. Connacht was left to the O Conchubhair family, and it remained a separate Irish kingdom until 1224. Ulster was ignored and left to John de Courcy. Most important of all, Prince John was made lord of Ireland, and Hugh de Lacy appointed his viceroy.

The decision taken at Oxford to proceed with the further enfeoffment of Ireland was undoubtedly facilitated by another explicit assertion of papal support for Henry II. Early in January 1177, the papal legate Vivian, cardinal-priest of St Stephen on the Coelian Hill, turned up in the north of Ireland for the purpose, according to Giraldus, of making peace between de Courcy and the Irish king of Ulster and of establishing that the annual tribute should be paid to the English. At first de Courcy imprisoned the legate for his pains, but he later released him on orders from FitzAudelin and escorted the cardinal to Dublin. There, on 13 March 1177, at a synod of bishops, the cardinal legate proclaimed the rights of the king of the English in Ireland and the confirmation of these rights by the sovereign pontiff. Both clergy and people were further warned, under pain of anathema, not to repudiate their fidelity to the king. Giraldus further adds that since the Irish were wont to hide their provisions under the cloak of sanctuary in churches, the English were given the right to extract them by force.

The years after 1177 were spent by new grantees in trying to establish themselves in their lands and by the Irish in fierce if uncoordinated resistance. Already the signs of future stalemate were evident. In some of the early Norman 'kingdoms' the new landowners and the Irish tenantry had already grown close together. It was fear of this development, and the suspicion that he might shelve his English allegiance and throw in his lot with Irish aspirations, that induced Prince John to dismiss Hugh de Lacy as his viceroy in 1184, and appoint John de Courcy in his place. In 1172 King Henry II had feared something similar from the Earl Richard, and he had established Hugh de Lacy as a counterweight in Meath. In 1204-05 King John suspected John de Courcy of a similar imprudence and used one of Hugh de Lacy's sons to oust de Courcy from Ulster. Later still, in 1210, King John sought the aid of the pardoned de Courcy to destroy the same de Lacy son who had since been granted the de Courcy earldom in Ulster.

Prince John was sent to visit his Irish dominion in 1185. He was accompanied by a heavyweight of legal talent in Ranulf Glanville, by Giraldus and by another wave of grantees. New charters were granted to Bertram de Verdun, William de Burgo, Theobald Walter, Roger Pippard, Philip de Worcester, John Comyn the first Anglo-Norman archbishop of Dublin and others. According to Giraldus one of the immediate effects of the visit was to drive a deeper wedge between the Irish and the English crown. The Annals briefly describe the visit:

The son of the king of England, i.e. John son of Henry II, came to Ireland with a fleet of sixty ships. He took possession of Dublin and Leinster, and

47

erected castles at Tibraghny and Ardfinnan, out of which he plundered Munster. But his people were defeated with great slaughter by Domnal O Briain. The son of the king then returned to England, to complain of Hugh de Lacy, who had prevented the Irish kings from sending him either tribute or hostages.

The visit of Prince John brought the first cycle of the Norman presence, from the point of view of the English monarchy, to the end of its first full turn. The complaints of loyal chroniclers like Giraldus emphasise the point. For him, Prince John should have been out fighting the Saracens and not the Christian Irish. When the prince ridiculed the Irish who came to do him homage, and let their beards be pulled in derision, he drove them further away from loyalty to the crown and strengthened the resistance of the three kings of Cork, Limerick and Connacht. He did further harm by giving away to a band of newcomers the land of the Irish who might have been induced to come to terms. Lastly the calibre of the latest wave of invaders, who now controlled the royal towns and garrisons, left a lot to be desired. As a result, concludes Giraldus, the country in 1185 was in a state of strife and turmoil. But if Prince John offended the native Irish when he came over, he distrusted the established Norman barons as well. By the time he became king, his fixed policy was to reduce the older baronage in Ireland, and replace it with more recent blood from England.[5]

The result was a slowdown in the Norman advance that soon turned into a stalemate – 'the real disaster of

Irish history. For the Normans could not rule the country themselves, but they were strong enough to prevent anyone else from ruling it, so that it was more disunited than it had ever been under tribal rule. The stalemate could have been ended by the extension of English rule to the Irish . . . but this would also have stopped the further extension of the invasion, which from the invaders' point of view was unthinkable. That they themselves could be exploited in the same way by later waves of invaders of course did not occur to them. It is the tragedy of colonialism that it is self-perpetuating, and that each generation of exploiters considers the previous one fair game.'[6]

3

Two Churches

The Norman occupation of Ireland was far less complete than the Norman occupation of England. As a consequence two different political, legal and social communities grew into existence side by side – the one centred mainly in Dublin around the colonial governor and depending to a great extent on a continuous infusion of fresh blood from England, the other formed by the mass of *aratores* and lower strata in the territories claimed by the Anglo-Normans as well as of the entire communities of the unoccupied areas.

The existence of the two different traditions is clearly seen in developments in the Christian Church. The coming of the Normans might plausibly be expected to produce new and strong support for the native reform movement. And to some extent it did. But something much more fundamental happened with the importation of the 'customs of the English Church'; a different concept of what the Church itself was, was brought in at the same time.

In the Irish understanding of things there was little place for corporate notions in general and they understood only a very modified idea of sovereignty. For all that a diocesan establishment had been roughly worked out before the Normans came, this did not mean the adoption of a corporate notion of the Church with the full political, economic and social implications of medieval England or Europe. Just as there was little idea of kingdom or state with an evolving concept of universal human sovereignty, equally in Christian matters the ideas of authority and power which were implied in the European idea of the Church as a monolithic human corporation were quite foreign to the native people. The absence of such a corporate concept is clear in the minimal inclination of twelfth- and thirteenth-century Irish Christians towards the crusading spirit which sought to eliminate or convert their religious rivals by force – the very idea which the Anglo-Normans used to justify their invasion. For the future this difference was to cause a fundamental area of misunderstanding with both the English and Anglo-Irish on the one hand, and with the papacy on the other. The clergy in Irish society formed a very distinct but integral part of the community, having taken over the social niche held from time immemorial by the druids and learned men. In return for their sacerdotal services and the sacraments, they received the traditional dues from their Christian clients and in no sense had they become mere appendages of a clerical and lay nobility. They might still invoke the curse of Bridget or Ciaran on those who injured them, but they did not depend on the power of their noble superiors for their protection.

The existence of two separate Churches becomes apparent within a few years of the Norman invasion.

Giraldus Cambrensis mentions them specifically in his account of the provincial Council of Dublin in 1186.[1] Pope Clement III recognised the division in 1190 when he appointed William of Ely as legate for England, Wales 'and that part of Ireland in which Prince John, count of Mortain, and brother of the king himself, has jurisdiction.'[2] At this time, Giraldus' friend Matthew O hEnni, archbishop of Cashel, was papal legate in Ireland. Pope Innocent III (1198-1216) lamented the continuous war and dissension 'between English and Irish' over ecclesiastical appointments and position.[3] Towards the end of his pontificate he condemned those 'clerics and ecclesiastical persons' who freely communicated with those excommunicated by the English and Anglo-Irish prelates for rising up against the king of England. The English archbishop of Dublin was told to suppress the conspiracies and secret movements against the king in Ireland.[4] Taken in conjunction with the general tone of Pope Innocent III's correspondence, it is plain that here the Pope was referring not only to the incipient nationalism, but also to the fact that Irish Churchmen did not recognise ecclesiastical censure, common canonical procedure, and other ingredients of the corporate Church.

The division is reflected in the papal registers. In the first decades of the thirteenth century, letters addressed to English prelates ruling Irish dioceses are frequently registered in the section entitled *Anglia*, while those to native Irish bishops are registered under *Hibernia*.

The correspondence of Pope Honorius III (1216-1227) shows a heightening state of tension. English law was manipulated to discriminate against the natives. The

English archdeacon of Armagh, Luke Netterville, censured an Irish priest in the absence of the archbishop. The priest had been unjustly accused of homicide by four bribed witnesses, three of whom were minors: the court demanded that the defence produce 58 priest witnesses from the same diocese who spoke the priest's language.[5]

On 6 August 1220 Honorius III condemned the English custom whereby Irish clerics were excluded from ecclesiastical preferment.[6] Two days later the Pope condemned a further abuse whereby the Irish were discriminated against in the administration of justice and controversies over ownership.[7] Inability to speak the invader's language was enough to ruin an Irishman's case. A letter dated 19 March 1221 reveals the two traditions entirely at variance with one another. The problem was a complaint from the archbishop of Cashel, an Irishman, concerning the property of the church of Cashel which had been sequestered by English magnates with the full support of the English king. The Pope in his reply outlined the attitude of both the king and the archbishop. The king defended his action according to English law which, he reminds the Pope, was introduced into Ireland when 'the English entered Ireland at the command of the Apostolic See, and subjected that land to the obedience of the Roman Church.' The Irish simply had to be discriminated against 'because of their ferocity.' Besides, the truth of the matter, said the king, was that 'the possessions of both clerics and barons, as well as others, which were not protected by garrisoned castles were uninhabitable for the English because of the almost continuous wars between English and Irish.' The contention of the archbishop on the other hand was based on ideas of justice and religious freedom which plainly were out of accord with the presuppositions of English society and the position of the king in the medieval Church.[8]

In 1224 Honorius III again repudiated the continued abuse whereby Irish clerics were excluded by English statute from promotion.[9] As time went on the situation deteriorated. For Pope Innocent IV (1243-1254) the Irish question entered the wider context of relations between *Sacerdotium* and *Regnum*. In Ireland itself the gap between the Anglo-Irish Church and the *ecclesia inter Hibernos* was widening.

The ecclesiastical partition was only a reflection of the wider cultural divison. In 1223 for example, the royal justiciar was instructed by the king that 'in land inhabited by Irishmen boundaries shall be made according to the custom of Ireland, and in land inhabited by Englishmen according to the custom of England.'[10] A consciousness of separate identity is apparent in such new native titles as 'king of all the Irish of Ireland'.[11] The banding together 'of all the Irish' in conspiracy against foreign authority – often abetted by earlier colonists who had gone native – was a common complaint of the king's representative in Dublin during the second and third decades of the thirteenth century.[12]

In terms of political organisation, pre-Norman Ireland was chaotically fragmented. Yet the arrival of the 'foreigners' was to show that there was more unity, of a cultural, if intangible, nature, than the political chaos would lead an observer to imagine. Although this unity or communion would rarely show itself in political terms, the churchmen and the poets – inheritors of the traditions from druids and learned men – found a common bond with which the outsiders could not come to terms. The imaginative, concrete and backward look preserved and perpetuated this cultural non-territorial unity against the philosophical and juridical notions of the highly organised society of medieval Europe.

At first glance the customs of the English Church, which the king introduced at the Council of Cashel, might be thought to coincide with the aims of the Irish canonical reorganisation; in fact these customs cloaked an understanding of the visible Church which was foreign to the Irish mind. What little we know of the native synods of this period, Kells in 1152, Mellifont in 1157, Bri mhic Taidh near Trim in 1158, Dervor in 1161, Clane in 1162, Lismore in 1166, Athboy in 1167, Armagh in 1171, Birr in 1174 and Clonfert in 1179 as well as the entries from the Annals, show an individuality and absence of abstract thinking which make a man's relations with his God and his fellows much more likely to depend on the concrete situation or traditional pact than on the details of an imported, and therefore unreal, social system. Whether in the method of convening, the membership or the legislation, the Irish councils bear little resemblance to contemporary synods in England or continental Europe.

The Norman, and subsequently Anglo-Irish Church, on the other hand, was much more a visibly unified structure, in which sometimes king and prelates had barely distinguishable functions. Unlike the *ecclesia inter Hibernos*, the Anglo-Irish Church had a corporate headquarters in Dublin, although prelates from other English strongholds such as Waterford, Ferns, Limerick, often held official posts in the colonial government also. The tone was set by King John who made a major grant to 'the archbishop of Dublin and his successors who are not Irishmen.'[13]

The coming into being of two different Christian Churches does not mean that they can both be clearly distinguishable at all times in subsequent centuries. There was the inevitable overlapping. As an immediate consequence of the Norman invasion, the papacy, both as the centralised organ of the institutional Church and as the see of the successor (*comarba*) of Peter, was brought into closer contact with the island. To this institution and source of Christian teaching the two Churches gave common allegiance for the time being. But when the Reformation came, it is noticeable that it was the less obviously canonical of the two traditions which perpetuated the Irish Catholic Church, while the other became the Anglican Church and took with it, as for example in Dublin, much of the structural trappings of the medieval Roman tradition – the cathedrals, medieval parish boundaries, churches and prebends.

4

THE ANGLO-IRISH CHURCH

The Anglo-Irish Church was an offshoot of the Church
in England, and its foundation inevitably followed, not
so much from the coming of the Norman barons, as from
the English royal rights in Ireland. Its government and
internal administration was possibly more in keeping with
universal canonical requirements than were the traditions
of the *ecclesia inter Hibernos*, yet it was essentially tied to
the English crown. The first act in the establishment of
the Anglo-Irish Church was made in 1181, when Henry
II summarily appointed John Comyn, an English judge
and archdeacon, to replace Laurence O'Toole as archbishop of Dublin. It was really founded by Prince John,
when as lord of Ireland, he visited his lordship in 1185.

The trouble with the imported notion of the Church
was that, for all its detailed organisation and mass of
juridical concepts, it was subject to tremendous pressure
from widely different sources. Like the Church in
England, although as time went on to a lesser degree, it
was the arena for the struggle between the king and the
papacy. The wealth and power of its top officials made
the highest offices the object of purely secular ambition,

or like any important civil service post, a reward for political loyalty. Its secular jurisdiction made impossible demands on bishops and prelates who were conscious of their pastoral responsibility. Not all the turmoil and violence in Church affairs which followed in the wake of the invasion can therefore be directly attributed to the individual foreign prelates and Anglo-Norman barons, or even to the king. The cause of this new kind of disturbance was partly the understanding of the Church itself which the newcomers brought with them.

John Comyn was a new being on the Irish scene. He was the first state prelate who owed his ecclesiastical office to the king. His office combined secular as well as spiritual jurisdiction, and courts for both. He held ample lands from the king and rich revenues. He was an important member of the king's council in Ireland. Yet notionally his appointment depended upon the successor of Peter and his behaviour upon the mandate to the Apostles.

After his appointment by the king's council in 1181 he went to Italy for consecration at the hands of the Pope. He took advantage of his visit to get full papal confirmation of his rights and of the possessions of the see of Dublin. He stayed in England after his return until 1184 when Henry II 'sent Archbishop John of Dublin to Ireland about the beginning of August to prepare the way for his son's arrival.'[1] It was during the visit of Prince John in the following year that a beginning was made in the establishment of the Anglo-Irish Church.

Within weeks of his arrival, Prince John was making wholesale grants and offers – of land, and both temporal and spiritual jurisdiction – to his followers and liegemen.

The most spectacular grant was the see of Glendalough to the archbishop of Dublin.[2] It took some years and a further grant from Prince John in 1192 before the diocese of Glendalough was suppressed and incorporated into the archdiocese of Dublin, but already in 1185 the tone was set for a new Church organisation dependent upon the English king. Among other things, Giraldus Cambrensis tells us, Prince John offered him either of the two vacant sees of Leighlin or Ferns.[3] The extant charters issued by Prince John from 1185 until he became king in 1199, and by his principal barons and representatives, show the Anglo-Irish Church put on a firm economic basis.

For all that he was a new type of churchman, and the prisoner of an alien system, the activities of John Comyn often correspond with the highest aims of the native reform party. Within three months of Prince John's departure, Comyn presided over a provincial council of Dublin. It was attended by the suffragans and major religious superiors of the province, and it opened on *Laetare* Sunday, 30 March 1186. Most of the participating churchmen were certainly Irish, but the detail shown in the legislation and the fact that it was so rapidly confirmed by the Pope betray English organisation and efficiency.

The text of the decrees of this council come to us in a letter of confirmation from Pope Urban III.[4] The manuscript source for the text is badly mutilated and there are some gaps in it. The substance of the decrees is clear for the most part, and the following translation fills in some of the more obvious gaps. Anything in square brackets is emendation by the translator.

Starting, therefore, with the altar, to which without neglect or fault, reverence is first and foremost due in the Church of God, we prohibit and under pain of suspension from orders and benefice forbid any priest to celebrate Mass, as has been the ancient custom of this country, on a wooden table. In monastery and baptismal churches the entire altar is to be of stone: if sufficient stone is not available to cover the entire altar-table, at least an altar-stone is to be inserted in the table where the Body of the Lord is to be consecrated: this stone is to be of such dimensions that during the consecration it can contain five crosses interspaced from each other and that it extends beyond the stand of the widest chalice. In oratories and chantry chapels where of necessity the altar is made of wood, the altar-stone, of the same size, is to be inserted into the wooden table and on this Mass is to be celebrated. Two altar-cloths are to be used, the top one – which is blessed – to cover the table of the altar, the other to cover the front of the altar right down to the base. These cloths are to be clean and without blemish so that from the cleanness and integrity of those who offer, the holiness of what is brought together to be sanctified is shown forth. Chalices in monastery and wealthier churches are to be made of gold or silver; in poorer churches the chalice may be of tin, but it must always be clean and in good condition. The host which bring us the Lamb without stain, alpha and omega, should be so fine, pure and immaculate that they indicate [the subject of?] the sacrifice, which nourishes the spirit rather than the body. The water is to be mixed with the wine with moderation so that the wine does not lose its natural taste or colour. [There follow some lines with gaps dealing with] the necessity for clean covers [for chalices? or ciboria?], a prescription to erect a sacrarium of stone or wood, with a hollow from which a channel runs directly into the ground, so that after sacred communion the fingers of the priest can be washed lest that in offering the sacrifice [particles become attached to his fingers] and that these particles washed away in water will not be trodden under foot or be defiled by contact with anything unclean.

Since among all the sacraments of the Christian religion, baptism is to be first in effect and in time, and to be given to all without differentiation as to age, sex or condition, it is decreed that in all baptismal churches a fixed baptistry, made of wood or stone, is to be erected in the middle of the church, or in some suitable place where the paschal procession can pass around it: the interior is to be lined with lead to keep it clean, the top is to be open and broad, and the bottom is to have an exit from which a channel runs, for the escape of the blessed water and consecrated chrism that has been used in baptising, into mother earth where it is absorbed. It is also decreed that old and worn vestments and altar-cloths are to be burned and the ashes thrown into this channel in the baptistry to be buried in the bowels of the earth. It is furthermore forbidden that the vessel used to pour water in baptism be used for any other human use, for it is entirely unworthy that what has been set aside for divine service should be converted to human use.

Cemeteries should be dedicated especially by bishops so that, by the patronage of the saints and the prayers of the faithful who visit, the souls of those who are buried there would be helped before the Lord. It is excessively cruel that the souls of the faithful should be defrauded of a great benefit through neglect by those from whom they ought rather to receive assistance on grounds both of humanity and of piety. For this reason we prohibit under pain of anathema that anyone should bury the bodies of the dead in any alleged cemetery unless it be quite clear, through written proof or the word of trustworthy witnesses, that it has been blessed by a bishop, not only as a sanctuary for the living but also for the burial of the dead. In a cemetery so dedicated no person is to be buried by a layman without the presence of a priest, for to him who regenerates, nourishes and absolves the living, who restores them by sacred viaticum, to him also falls the office to commend with proper rites the departed soul to God and to commit his body to the earth.

It is disgraceful and contrary to both divine and human law that the members be in disharmony with the head and that inferiors take away from the honour due to superiors. Consequently we prohibit by every means that Mass be celebrated in chapels constructed by laymen to the injury of mother churches, without the permission of the bishop of the diocese and of the pastor of the mother church.

Since among other things in which the clergy of Ireland have excelled, the esteem for the virtues of chastity has always hitherto flourished, it would indeed be absurd and shameful, if, in our time, we – however unworthy – who have undertaken the care of souls under a most holy Pope and a most Christian king, should stain the lily of purity either by our own negligence or by the foul contagion of strangers, and that the religion of the many should be corrupted by the examples of a few incontinent people. For this reason under pain of suspension from office and benefice we strictly forbid that any priest, deacon or subdeacon should have any woman in his house under the pretext of necessary service or under any such just pretext, unless she be his mother or blood sister or be of such an advanced age that all suspicion of unlawful concubinage would be removed.

Since the crime of simony is known as one of the most detestable before God and man, all the more reason why ecclesiastics should take greater care to avoid it. For this reason we forbid priests under pain of suspension from office and benefice, to exact a fee for the administration of Extreme Unction, for the burial of the dead, for blessing [blank] or any other [blank]: if any layman, inspired by the devil, attempts to impose such a fee, he is declared subject to major excommunication until he has made satisfaction for such enormous excesses.

None are to be more severely corrected by canonical censure that those who, since they are called by the Lord to rule and care of the church, by blind avarice seek to trample ecclesiastical liberty. Therefore [blank] renewing the decrees of the holy fathers we declare that any cleric who accepts an ecclesiastical benefice from lay hands, and who after three warnings does not renounce the possessions which he has received by means of such intrusion, is to be smitten by sentence of anathema and to be wholly deprived of that benefice.

Since we are prohibited by evangelical teaching to ply our sickle in another's harvest and following the authority of the canons, we forbid that any bishop should presume to ordain a candidate from another diocese without letters of commendation from his proper bishop or archdeacon or to promote anyone to orders without assigning a definite title to a benefice, for it is shameful and reprehensible that the ministers of the Lord's table should have [to beg?] in the streets. For this purpose of correcting an illicit custom we strictly forbid that anyone be promoted to two sacred orders on the same day: [there follows a statement of the outcome if such a practice continues].

[The next decree deals with matrimony and so much of it is lost that the full meaning is obscure. There is a reference to] a praiseworthy custom of the Irish people [and it appears to indicate a healthier attitude to marriage than other contemporary evidence from outside would admit] after contracting matrimony the partners, being bound more strictly to the observance of God's laws, are wont [long blank space] from robberies and other crimes [blank]: [there follows a reference to those] living in fornication are to be compelled [blank] to good spouses [blank] greater profit for [their?] souls as compared with other nations.

We declare [blank] so that nobody born of concubinage, after the promulgation of this decree, is to be promoted to sacred orders, nor to be considered as heirs to its father or mother, unless subsequently [the parents] shall be united in legitimate wedlock. [There follows a statute laying down penalties] for those who continue to openly live a life of fornication.

Since therefore the Almighty, who has deigned to give us all we have, keeps back a tithe for needy souls, not as a levy for Himself but for the profit of those giving it, following the statutes of the holy fathers we renew the law that tithes are to be paid to mother churches on grain, hay, the breeding of animals, flax and wool, fruit of gardens and orchards and on all things that are renewed from year to year. According to Augustine and Ambrose tithes are to be paid, not only on those things we have enumerated, but also on military exploits, trade, craftsmanship and hunting. But in this part of the world, the longer men show themselves unwilling to pay tithes to God, so much the longer will they be bound in future to seek pardon for their past contumacy by paying all the more. Whoever then presumes to act in this way, if after three warnings he doesn't make satisfaction, he is to be smitten with a sentence of anathema.

The outbreak of a new disorder compels us to devise new remedies: this concerns those archers who sell their warlike skills not for the defence of the people but for shameful gain and rapine, and thereby intensify their ingrained evil by the filth of repeated crime: we decree that in every parish on every Sunday, with lighted candles and solemn pealing of bells, [ecclesiastical censure is to be read out against those] who inflict such violence and rapine both in what has been committed to their attention and in other things, and they are to be deprived of Christian burial at death.

Even in Archbishop John Comyn's provincial synod mention is found of opposing traditions, and Giraldus Cambrensis confirms that the danger to Irish clerical chastity came from the Anglo-Normans.

The Anglo-Normans were also responsible for the establishment of a secular clergy – at least in the form which in fact came into being. Some notion of a secular clergy must have been in the minds of the Irish reformers who met at Kells in 1152, but as Giraldus tells us a decade and a half after the invasion, the Irish bishops were still largely recruited from the monasteries. Whether it was to combat this tendency, or in imitation of developments in England, Archbishop John Comyn established a secular diocesan chapter in Dublin to compete with the monastic chapter at Holy Trinity. In 1192, attended by numerous Irish bishops and prelates, he consecrated St Patrick's cathedral and established a secular collegiate church. The tone of the deed also expresses the attitude of the newcomers to native Christianity.

> John by the grace of God minister to the Church in Dublin. Since learning flourishes throughout the world and teachers of both divine and human lore are numerous in every kingdom except Ireland, and wishing to provide for the less erudite simplicity of the Irish people, we have decided by the authority of God and with the consent of the Holy See of Rome and of our prince, John count of Mortain, to make St Patrick's Dublin a prebendal church and to establish in it a college of clerics of approved life and learning.'[5]

Before Comyn's death in 1212 the secular canons of St Patrick's had gained rights in the election of his successor.

For the most part, John Comyn's energies were directed to enlarging the estates and lands of his see, just like any secular lord. Grants of liberties and immunities plus the shrewd economic deals of Comyn and his successors made the archbishop of Dublin one of the most privileged royal subjects in the Anglo-Irish community.

The Anglo-Normans had an equally decisive effect on the development of religious orders. A fair sprinking of the new medieval religious communities had been founded, largely in the province of Dublin, before their arrival. But they brought a distinctive new genre of religious community.

Again the imported ideas of the coenobitical life were closely dependent upon the economic and social life of England. New Benedictine and Cistercian foundations followed in the wake of the conquerors, and an even greater number of new houses of the various forms of Augustinian canons. Some of these new communities were founded or moulded on early Irish foundations which had disintegrated in the new social and economic atmosphere. Most were new foundations, typical medieval corporations which soon amassed great wealth. The monatic foundations of John de Courcy in the land he conquered in the north are a pattern of what happened in most of the colonised areas.

As soon as he forged his way into Ulster in 1177, de Courcy appointed the first foreigner to rule an Irish see. Bishop Reginald appears in the diocese of Connor within months of de Courcy's incursion. In the neighbouring diocese of Down, a Bishop Malachy, whatever his origin, was equally submissive. But it was in the field of monastic foundations that de Courcy's innovations are most notable.[6] All of them were made with imported religious. He began with the cathedral of Down. The Irish organisation – possibly a chapter of Augustinian canons regular – was replaced by a Benedictine foundation. The new monks at St Patrick's (the name was changed from Holy Trinity by John de Courcy) were brought from St Werburgh's at Chester, and William de Etleshale appointed the first prior. The bishop of the diocese retained the title abbot. Then in quick succession two more Benedictine foundations were made at St Andrew in Ards with monks from Stoke Courcy, and on the island of

Nendrum with monks from St Mary's York and its dependent priory St Bees. Cistercian foundations were made at Iniscourcy from Furness and at Grey Abbey near Newtownards from Holm Cultrum in Cumberland. A Premonstratensian house was established at St Mary's in Carrickfergus and the *Cruciferi* were given the priory of St John the Baptist in Down. The priory of St Thomas the Martyr was founded at Tobberglorie in Down as a house of canons regular dependent on St Mary's at Carlisle. Various land grants were also made to other Anglo-Norman foundations throughout the colonised territories by de Courcy, e.g. to St Thomas in Dublin. But all of these foundations belonged to the new tradition, and there was little or no communion with native Irish Christianity. John de Courcy himself, the founder and great benefactor of so many imported monastic establishments, was known among the Irish as 'the destroyer of the churches of Ireland.' When he left the north some of his foundations were unable to outlive his political protection; the Premonstratension house at Carrickfergus, for example, was abandoned shortly after 1224.

This new type of monastic establishment and the pattern of founding them was paralleled elsewhere. At first the common loyalty within the different religious orders was more powerful than the divergence between the Anglo-Norman and Irish ecclesiastical traditions, and Benedictine, Cistercian and Augustinian sister-houses flourished in Anglo-Norman and Irish territories. But within decades a new pattern evolved, with each order tending to split into two opposing factions – Anglo-Irish communities of Cistercians, for example, on the one hand,

and native Irish communities on the other. The split which the Cistercian Visitator found in 1227, was reflected in every order, and the statues which excluded those, who spoke the Irish language only, from Anglo-Irish monasteries, tended to canonise the division between the two Churches.[7]

The period between the murder of Archbishop Becket in 1170 and the submission of King John to the Pope in 1213 was a critical one for the Church in England, not only because the question of *sacerdotium* and *regnum* was being worked out but also because basic questions of ecclesiastical structure and discipline were being tackled by churchmen and statesmen alike. The Fourth Lateran Council of 1215, to a large degree, merely codified what had already been worked out in the previous decades of great tension. Although the structure and discipline of the Anglo-Irish Church was imported from England, the growing pains of the Church in England were barely reflected in the establishment of the Anglo-Irish ecclesiastical tradition. Far more than the Church in England, the ecclesiastical structure imported by the colonists waas identified with the monarchy; it depended on royal support for survival in alien surroundings. Apart from John Comyn, who spent nearly half his thirty one years as archbishop of Dublin in exile, for his opposition to royal interference, Anglo-Irish churchmen were mainly adjuncts of the colonial government. Consequently the Anglo-Irish Church in the twelfth and thirteenth centuries lacked the vigour of English Church life and was at best a pale reflection, censored by royal power, of developments in the mother-church. Well might Swift have wondered, centuries later, how it was that every virtuous English bishop translated to Ireland was murdered on Hounslow Health and his place taken by a highwayman.

The Constitutions of Clarendon of 1164 more or less defined the attitude the royal government would take to the Church in Ireland. In practice this meant royal rights in ecclesiastical elections and over ecclesiastical property – problems concerning judicial procedures in relation to churchmen did not arise until later. These rights were acceptable for the most part to those in the Anglo-Irish tradition: to the native Irish they were incomprehensible. Where the two traditions clashed, as happened when an Anglo-Irish and an Irish candidate for a bishopric faced each other, physical power was usually the deciding factor. Consequently, with the notable exception of John Comyn, the activites of the churchmen in the Anglo-Irish tradition were principally aimed at expanding and consolidating their territorial sphere of influence, in alliance with the colonial government and the local magnates.

King Henry II was too busy controlling the early colonists and establishing an effective central government for them in Dublin to become deeply involved in Irish Church affairs. Besides, he appears to have accepted the injuctions of Pope Alexander III to protect and fortify the Irish hierarchy. His two appointments to bishoprics in Ireland – the habit of interference remained for all his good intentions – were in keeping with this spirit. Augustine, a local priest, was appointed to Waterford in 1175 and John Comyn was sent to Rome to have his appointment to Dublin confirmed. But under John, both before and after he became king, and during the minority of Henry III, the royal officials principally understood Irish ecclesiastical offices as adjuncts of the colonial government and fair game for the politically and economically ambitious.

Hamo de Valognes, the royal justiciar from 1196 to 1199, was rather typical. When Giraldus Cambrensis turned down Prince John's offer of the see of Leighlin in 1185, a certain John became bishop. This bishop died some time in 1197-98 and the abbot of the Cistercian monastery of Monasterevan was elected by the chapter of Leighlin to replace him. The justiciar, however, refused to recognise the election: he seized the cathedral and imprisoned the canons. The bishop-elect appealed to the papal legate who confirmed the election but refused to consecrate the new bishop for fear of Hamo de Valognes. The bishop-elect then set out for the papal curia where Pope Innocent III consecrated him. But meantime the justiciar had installed an excommunicated monk, who had been expelled from Canterbury, as bishop of Leighlin. The man imprisoned the archdeacon, forced him to resign his office and appointed a henchman of his own to replace him. Despite round condemnations by two Popes, and despite his excommunication, the intruded monk held on to the bishopric of Leighlin until his death in 1217.[8] Shortly before the Leighlin affair, Hamo de Valognes had seized the temporalities of the see of Dublin and banished the archbishop into exile.[9]

There were disputed elections in most of the dioceses of Ireland during the reign of King John. Where either one or the other of the two Church traditions had overall control, the disputes were settled without appeals to the papal curia. In dioceses and monasteries where the two traditions were battling it out for control, most of the disputes ended up on the Pope's desk. In Ross, a Norman successfully ousted an Irish monk who had been elected bishop by the diocesan chapter – despite a writ from the Pope confirming the choice of the chapter.[10] King John nominated three Norman candidates during the long vacancy in Armagh from 1202 to 1206: to two of them the king made an outright grant of the see. The Irish candidate, Echdonn mac Gille Uidhir the abbot of Bangor, who had been elected by the bishops of the northern province, spent over three years and a visit to the Pope before King John was obliged to recognise his promotion to the archbishopric.[11] Even that victory was short lived, for it appears that the new archbishop was forced to appoint an Anglo-Norman as archdeacon with right of succession. When the see of Cashel became vacant in 1206, the king instructed both the chapter and his justiciar to see to it that his nominee, Ailbe of Ferns, was appointed;[12] the following year in Limerick the chapter was not even informed: the king made an outright grant of the bishopric to Geoffrey, rector of Dungarvan, and instructed the justiciar to ensure that the clergy and people accepted Geoffrey as their new bishop.[13] In both these cases the king was unsuccessful, but a pattern was being set and the Anglo-Irish Church was tied more closely to the crown. After his submission to Pope Innocent III in 1213, there was little change in the king's policy. The following year, he instructed the justiciar, the chapter of Cork and the metropolitan in Cashel to appoint a royal nominee, Geoffrey White, to the see of Cork.[14] The most vivid pictures of the Anglo-Irish Church in action, and the opposition to it from the native Irish, are seen in an attempt to take over the native diocese of Lismore. The saga is worth recording in some detail.[15]

It was suggested at the Council of Kells, when the hierarchy was established in 1152, that some of the tiny bishoprics which were carried over from the monastic era might be absorbed by neighbouring dioceses. This pseudo-Isidorian decree became a convenient legal justification for the Anglo-Norman methods of expansion. The decree was used to justify the suppression of the Irish diocese of Glendalough and its absorption into the smaller diocese of Dublin. The metropolitan of the West, Felix O Ruadhain, who maintained his position as archbishop of Tuam only with the support of the government in Dublin, made a similar attempt to absorb the diocese of Mayo.

In the south, a series of Anglo-Irish bishops of Waterford made a determined effort to take over the native Irish bishopric of Lismore. Much of the countryside surrounding Waterford belonged to the diocese of Lismore. In the closing years of the twelfth century, an unnamed Anglo-Irish bishop of Waterford gathered a small force of armed men, occupied the cathedral of Lismore and banished the Irish bishop, Felix, from his diocese. The aggressor died in 1199, and the bishop of Lismore returned from exile. The next bishop of Waterford, Robert I, was a royal appointee who had been a member of King John's court. He arrived in Waterford in 1201 and immediately set about re-opening the offensive against Lismore. Once more Felix was banished. The bishop of Lismore was at this stage weary of the affair; first he appealed to the recently arrived legate, John, cardinal priest of Monte Celio, whom Innocent III had sent to look into the disturbed affairs in Ireland. Then suddenly Felix resigned. The legate took the easy way out and confirmed the union of the two sees of Waterford and Lismore, with Robert I as bishop of the united sees. But neither the legate nor Robert I had reckoned with the clergy and people of Lismore. They rejected the legate's decision, chose one of their own, a Cistercian abbot named Malachy, and planned an appeal to Rome. Bishop-elect Malachy and some of his clergy had barely set out on their journey to Italy when they were ambushed by an armed force led by the bishop of Waterford. Malachy was captured, severely beaten and thrown into prison, but the archdeacon of Lismore and some of the clergy managed to escape and make their way to Rome. There they were later joined by the bishop-elect who had in the meantime made good his escape from prison.

Pope Innocent III had Malachy consecrated and he sent the visitors home armed with letters from the curia at Anagni. One of these was addressed to the clergy and the people of Lismore enjoining obedience to their new bishop, Malachy. The other letter established an episcopal commission to ensure that Malachy was given possession of his see and that Bishop Robert I of Waterford was severely censured. The members of the commission were the archbishop of Tuam and the bishop of Ferns, both noted Anglo-Irish sympathisers, and the bishop of Kilmacduagh. There was no difficulty in carrying out the papal mandate as bishop Robert I died in the summer of 1204. Bishop Malachy established himself in Lismore.

The next bishop of Waterford was appointed by the personal intervention of King John. He was David the 'Welshman', a cousin of the justiciar Meiler FitzHenry and a royal official himself. In 1203 the king had granted him the church of Dungarvan, but he had remained at the court during the king's difficulties with France. He finally arrived in Ireland in 1205, and immediately organised yet another offensive against Lismore. Once again the bishop of that see was driven out, and once again Bishop Malachy took the road to Rome. A sympathetic Innocent III issued new instructions. This time a more favourable commission was appointed: it included the bishops of Cork and Killaloe and the archdeacon of Cashel. Malachy did not return to Ireland until late 1207. The judges-delegate set about their mandate with determination. Bishop David of Waterford was summoned to appear before them. Counter charges against the bishop of Lismore caused some delay. A new date for the hearing was set when suddenly another event summarily ended David the Welshman's personal interest in the proceedings. He was assassinated by the local Irish chief, Ua Faelain of the Deisi, over another matter in which he had offended the native people. The papal delegates installed Malachy in his bishopric at Lismore.

The see of Waterford remained vacant until King John visited Ireland in 1210. Bishop Robert II was appointed sometime after June of that year. Before his consecration, yet another attack was organised against Lismore and the bishop expelled. Despite the protests of Malachy, the archbishop of Cashel had Robert II consecrated. The archbishop made it clear that by his action he was not prejudicing the Waterford-Lismore issue: he was merely obeying King John. But the papal judges-delegate showed no such fears. They summoned Robert II to answer the charge of having had Bishop Malachy expelled and having taken violent possession of the see of Lismore. The judges reiterated that Lismore was from time immemorial a cathedral church, that Malachy had been canonically elected and validly consecrated, and that he had been unlawfully expelled. Robert II was found guilty, and although he refused to attend the hearing, he was commanded to pay for the temporal damages suffered by the bishop of Lismore. The bishop of Cork was authorised to execute the sentence. So, early in 1211, Bishop Malachy was once again installed in Lismore.

Some weeks later, on the Saturday before Passion Sunday, 19 March 1211, while Bishop Malachy was conferring Holy Orders in his cathedral, Bishop Robert II's armed posse, led by Roger Christopher, broke into the church. Malachy was dragged out, stripped of his vestments and clothes and carried off, with two of his assistant priests, to prison at Dungarvan. Bishop Robert himself helped the smith secure the iron fetters on Bishop Malachy's hands and feet.

News of the assault spread rapidly. It was not known at first that Bishop Robert II was personally involved. A synod was called jointly by the papal judges-delegate and by the archbishop of Cashel. Most of the southern bishops attended, including Robert II of Waterford. The unknown perpetrators of the outrage were excommunicated. Robert II in council, like his episcopal colleagues bearing lighted candle, assented to the sentence.

There were seven weeks of torture in store for Bishop Malachy before he escaped from Dungarvan Castle. On hearing his account of the event, the papal judges immediately summoned Robert II to appear before them. The latter at first denied his involvement, but reliable witnesses gave evidence against him. He then began to threaten the wrath of King John on the southern bishops if they proceeded with the case. Unimpressed, the judges determined to carry out a full canonical enquiry. A day was appointed for the trial in Limerick cathedral and witnesses were called. The bishop of Waterford had no defence and he again threatened the judges with the king's displeasure. When he failed to intimidate them, Robert II withdrew from the trial and secretly commissioned one of his clerics, a certain Thomas, to assassinate the bishop of Lismore. As Bishop Malachy emerged from the cathedral with the papers of the official sentence in his hands, the cleric Thomas approached, snatched the documents from the bishop's hands and lunged with his sword. The bishop of Lismore ducked just in time, the sword barely missed his head, and stuck in the door of the cathedral.

The cleric Thomas was excommunicated on the spot and thrown into prison. Bishop Robert II was forbidden to communicate with him. Nevertheless, we are told, the bishop of Waterford continued to minister to his cleric *tam in corporali quam in spirtuali*. He also refused to answer a summons from the ecclesiastical court. Robert II was then excommunicated.

The inherent weakness of the Anglo-Irish Church and its irrelevance except as an adjunct of the secular power is highlighted in the Waterford-Lismore dispute at this stage. Robert II, who had the support of the justiciar and the king, ignored the canonical proceedings and returned to his diocese. All the papal judges could do was report the matter to the Pope.

The answer of Innocent III was to appoint yet a third commission. This time it included the justiciar, the erstwhile excommunicated bishop of Norwich, John de Grey. His fellow judges were the bishops of Clonfert and Annaghdown. The new commission was simply told to restore the bishop of Lismore to his see, to ratify the excommunication of the bishop of Waterford, and to order him to come in person to Rome. Bishop Malachy was restored to Lismore, but Robert II of Waterford could not be tampered with in the external forum. His ecclesiastical authority depended on the king and the papal judges were powerless. By 1215 Robert II was, in the eyes of the world, the legitimate bishop of Waterford, free from all censure.

Lismore's troubles were eased with the death of King John. The regency council in England was much more dependent on papal support during the minority of Henry III, and two further papal mandates in favour of Lismore, in 1216 and 1218, were given sufficient respect to have Bishop Robert II of Waterford kept in check.

The tension between the two Church traditions came to a head during the minority of King Henry III, i.e. in the decade after 1216. Neither tradition was victorious over the other, but enduring attitudes were consolidated and each tradition became polarised. It was stalemate: at one extreme a government Church devoid of independent spiritual vigour, at the other extreme an unorganised spiritual heritage which soon became identified with the Irish language and later with Irish nationalism. King John was too close to events to see the naïveté of his complaint to Innocent III in 1202 that the bishops of Clogher, Clonmacnoise, Kells and Ardagh, and the archdeacon of Armagh showed an open desire to work against the 'king's right and dignity regarding the church of Armagh.'[16] But for Henry of London, the representative of the regency council in the government of Ireland, and John Comyn's successor as archbishop of Dublin, there were few illusions in the advice he gave regarding royal policy towards the Church.[17]

Henry of London, a member of the royal court, archdeacon of Stafford and faithful supporter of King John during the interdict and trouble with the papacy, came to Ireland a few months before John Comyn died, at the end of 1212. Within a short time he was back at the king's side in England to witness the formal submission to Innocent III on 15 May 1213, but by then he had become archbishop-elect of Dublin. After the king's death, he became the centre of the colonial government in Ireland. As archbishop (1213-28), as royal justiciar (1213-15 and 1221-24) and as papal legate (1217-20) it seemed for a time 'that he might make a radical change in the whole character of the Irish hierarchy, substituting English for Irish bishops in every diocese of the four provinces.'[18] Known to his tenants as 'flayer of serfs' he ruthlessly used his triple power to abolish Irish Christianity and substitute the Anglo-Irish Church. For ten years circumstances were in his favour. But he overplayed his hand, and in the long run served as a catalyst in driving a permanent wedge between the Anglo-Irish and native Irish religious traditions.

Henry of London was occupied with external affairs until the beginning of 1217. He was at King John's side during the crisis of 1215 which ended with the signing of *Magna Carta*, and shortly afterwards he went to Rome for the General Council of the Lateran which opened in November 1215. His most notable ecclesiastical activity in Ireland before he left was the attempt to intrude the king's nominee, Geoffrey White, into the see of Cork.

The three other archbishops and sixteen suffragans also attended the Fourth Lateran Council:[19] from the northern province, the bishops of Clonmacnoise, Down, Meath and Raphoe; from Leinster the bishops of Ferns and Kildare; from the south the bishops of Emly, Killaloe, Limerick, Ross and Waterford as well as the bishop-elect of Lismore; from Connacht the bishops of Achonry, Annaghdown, Killala and the bishop-elect of Mayo. It is impossible to divide these twenty prelates into two camps; even the committed government bishops – Down, Dublin, Emly, Limerick, Lismore, Meath, Tuam and Waterford – did not necessarily reflect the interests of the clergy and people.

Archbishop Henry of London spent twelve months in Rome 'where he was active on the king's behalf as leader of the English party in the divided Irish hierarchy.'[20] Innocent III was easily convinced of the utter incompetence and even lack of goodwill, in native Irish bishops. Sharp letters were issued to the latter deploring their attitude and Archbishop Henry was instructed to suppress their independent tendencies.[21] The native kings were represented as obstacles to ecclesiastical freedom, and the king of Connacht was instructed by the Pope to desist from such practices and to observe the statutes of the general council. To his own territory the archbishop of Dublin gave special attention. The suppression of Glendalough and its absorption into Dublin received papal confirmation – a manoeuvre greatly assisted by the favourable evidence of the archbishop of Tuam. Papal letters of protection and confirmation of property were issued to the archbishop and many of the institutions under his control. The imposition of English liturgical usage was endorsed. A decision in favour of the bishop of Ferns was got and entrusted to the safe hands of the archbishops of Dublin and Tuam. When Honorius III became Pope, the Anglo-Irish faction turned their attention to him before leaving the curia. A further confirmation of the suppression of Glendalough was obtained as well as more letters of protections and confirmation for rights and possessions. A decision in favour of the archbishop of Tuam and against the interests of the Irish diocese of Armagh was wangled from the Pope after the archbishop of Armagh had died in Rome. Henry of London got special powers to control the religious orders in his province. Honorius III was deeply committed to protecting the rights of the young king, Henry III, and there was no difficulty in convincing him that the Irish were a dire threat to English royal authority. Archbishop Henry 'in whose loyalty and prudence we have particular confidence' was given special powers to ensure fealty among the troublesome Irish. Presenting the affairs of Ireland in this light was Henry of London's speciality in his dealings with the papal curia and it was spectacularly successful for a few years. By April 1217 he had managed to have himself appointed papal legate for Ireland.

A letter to the justiciar of Ireland shortly before Archbishop Henry's return to Dublin defined his status in government and his responsibility for the affairs of the colony. 'Although we know that the presence in England of our venerable father Lord Henry, archbishop of Dublin, is most necessary to us and to our kingdom and that we can scarcely do without his counsel, nevertheless we are sending him to Ireland that he may visit and console his church which has been desolate for so long, and that he may strive with your help and counsel for the amendment of the state of Ireland and the execution of what needs to be done in your country.'[22] Two earlier mandates in the king's name exemplify the royal policy. On 14 January 1217, the justiciar, Geoffrey de Marisco, was instructed not to permit any Irishman to be elected or appointed to any cathedral church in Ireland since 'our land of Ireland' could be disturbed by such appointments. Three days later, another order was made bidding the justiciar not to permit any Irishman to be elected or promoted in future to any Irish see. The justiciar was to take counsel with the archbishop of Dublin and to use every means in his power to procure the election and promotion of the king's clerics and other honest English clerics when vacancies in bishoprics and other ecclesiastical offices should arise.[23]

Henry of London set to work in a businesslike manner. St Patrick's cathedral was put on a firm footing and a group of English canons given absolute control.[24] Then, apart from his property and financial deals on behalf of his see in Ireland, he bought a farm and a house in the town of Beaune in France for the use of the archbishops of Dublin and their agents passing to and fro on their way to the papal curia.[25] Clearly he intended making full use of the papal curia in furthering his aims.

During his period of power an Anglo-Irish candidate was installed in the diocese of Ardagh, in opposition to the Irish bishop, Donnchadh Ua Maoilciarain. In Ardfert and Killaloe the 1217 elections of native bishops according to Irish custom were summarily set aside and a brace of Anglo-Irish candidates 'violently installed'. In the case of Killaloe, the government nominee was Robert Travers, the nephew of the justiciar. Both were consecrated by the Anglo-Irish bishops of Emly, Limerick and Waterford.[26] In 1218-19 Anglo-Irish bishops succeeded in Armagh and Ossory, and the Pope had again to intervene in the dispute over Lismore and have an intruder expelled.

Happily for the Church in Ireland, Henry of London's ruthlessness and greed were not confined to his dealings with the native people. He fell foul of some Anglo-Irish ecclesiastics over matters of property and he had serious disputes with other royal officials. Meantime Donnchadh Ua Longargain, the archbishop of Cashel, had begun to lead a concerted native attempt to fight the government policy. Pressure began to build against the archbishop of Dublin. In March 1220, a letter from the king reminded him that it was expected that he be as solicitous in preserving the king's rights as he himself wishes the king to be in guarding the archbishop's liberties.[27] In Rome there were appeals against him from the bishops of Killaloe, Ardfert and from the archbishop of Cashel.

Donnchadh Ua Longargain's mission was concerned with the whole question of English rule in Ireland. He had suffered personally, and certain possessions of the see of Cashel had never, since his consecration, been given to him. In a belated attempt to repair the situation, Henry of London warned the authorities in England towards the end of 1219, and again early in 1220, that the archbishop of Cashel was about to protest personally to the Pope, after he had laid his diocese under interdict. Henry advised that all his possessions be restored to the archbishop of Cashel immediately, since his personal appeal to the Pope might be the cause of disturbance in Ireland.

How right Henry of London was! He himself was one of the first to suffer. On 6 July 1220 the Pope informed him that he should no longer be papal legate. A special legate *a latere*, James, papal chaplain and penitentiary, was being sent to replace him.[28] A series of papal condemnations of English ecclesiastical policy followed and the new legate was instructed to see that English abuses were remedied. James was directed to revoke unlawful alienation of ecclesiastical property, to denounce the English custom in Ireland whereby Irish clerics were excluded from ecclesiastical preferment and to abolish the corrupt practice whereby the Irish were discriminated against in court proceedings. Papal protection was afforded the king of Connacht. The legate was further instructed to oust the two Anglo-Irish intruders in the bishoprics of Killaloe and Ardfert.[29]

The mission of the archbishop of Cashel made an impression at the papal curia. The Popes became far less

easily influenced by English and Anglo-Irish representation, and further condemnations of Anglo-Irish abuses
were to follow. Irish representation met more favourable
hearing. But few realised the gulf that separated the two
traditions. Honorius III tried to overcome the deadlock
in the Cashel vacancy of 1223-24 by appointing an
outsider of considerable fame, Michael Scot, to the see.
But this appointment – the first papal provision in Ireland
– failed because of the candidate's ignorance of the Irish
language. The reality of the situation was expressed in
the report by the Irish annalists on the mission of the
papal legate, James. 'James Penciail came to Ireland as
legate from Rome, to settle and arrange ecclesiastical
affairs; and he collected horseloads of gold and silver from
the clerics of Ireland through simony, and departed from
Ireland in the same year.'[30]

We are right back in the spirit of ninth-century Ireland:

Pilgrim, take care your journey's not in vain,
a hazard without profit, without gain;
the King you seek you'll find in Rome, it's true,
but only if he travels on the way with you.[31]

5

IRISH CHRISTIANITY

The lack of fixed ecclesiastical boundaries and the absence of an overall corporate expression severely limits any attempt to describe a consecutive history of the *ecclesia inter Hibernos*. Whatever its evolution as a social body, that faith and Church which had been embraced in the fifth century defies simple structural description in the twelfh. It might be called a state of mind with an uncanny knack of discriminating, largely unconsciously, between the object of its traditional belief and the complexities of social and political life. The one it did not analyse too deeply for rational justification, the other had consequently little philosophical foundation. Preoccupation with dogma took little of its time − yet there was no question of doctrinal heterodoxy. Anselm of Canterbury suggested that it might be schismatic; there had indeed been a healthy individuality and structural independence inherent in it since the time of St Columbanus.

The mind behind this Christianised druidism has been defined as concrete and imaginative rather than abstract and rationalist. It was practical as opposed to theoretical, yet idealist rather than pragmatic. Irish Christianity, like Irish literature of the time, has all the intangibility of an intuitive culture which found many of its ideals in a past heroic age.

That great canonist and statesman, Pope Innocent III, found it impossible to understand. He was the epitome of everything that Irish Christianity was not – and only divine faith bound them in the same Church. At the end of his pontificate he sent a general letter of disgust to the Irish prelates. Only a summary of his letter remains, but it expresses the Pope's mind. 'The prelates of Ireland are reprimanded because they settle church matters without regard for the facts, without thought and without taking the advice of competent people. They are told not to settle these cases in future without specialist's counsel.'[1]

Yet the contrast with the outside world is not one of sheer primitive backwardness and obscurantism as opposed to sophistication and liberal ideas. The pre-Norman religious reform had already left its mark. 'The transformation which the reformers had brought about in the life of the Irish church did not prevent a conscious effort by Irish scholars to record their traditions; indeed, the sense of their otherness may have further stimulated antiquarian activity. In the twelfth century *The Book of the Taking* (*Lebor Gabala*) systematised the accepted 'history' of early Ireland, probably on the basis of an eighth century original. The scribes put together a great mass of miscellaneous material in three great manuscript collections; *The Book of the Dun Cow* (*Lebor na hUidre*) transcribed at Clonmacnoise, *The Book of Leinster* compiled by Aed abbot of Terryglass, and a manuscript now in the Bodleian Library, Rawl. B. 502, the provenance of which is unknown. The masters who determined the compilations did not hesitate to include purely secular material. *The Book of the Taking* defends the arts of *eolas* and *filidecht* (learning and poetry), for 'though the Faith came, these arts were not put away, for they are good.'[2]

There are signs too that this very different society, while retaining its distinctive characteristics, could adapt itself to progressive influences from without. Legal documentation and diplomatic practice show that the native Irish could innovate to suit their own customs. *Notitiae* and charters in the vernacular are extant from about 1140 and show a consistent development until 1161. The *ars notaria* itself was adapted to suit Irish legal notions. The continental witnesses are replaced by the Irish legal equivalent, sureties. The inability to alienate property without the consent of the *fine* is expressed in the consent of a *concilium* of named relatives. The symbolic invocation occurs in a Gaelic charter of 1133. During the twelfth century Latin was used in documents: Muirchertach Ua Lochlain, *rex totius Hiberniae*, issued documents in both Latin and Irish. A *cancellarius regis* appears in the documents of Diarmuid Mac Murchadha, king of Leinster, and a *cancellarius* of the high-king, Ruaidhri O Conchobhair, was sent on the diplomatic mission to Windsor in 1175.[3]

The influence of the Hildebrandine reform shows a more profound social and cultural change. The developments in the rights and status of women that took place in the post-classical period of Irish law would seem to have been the result, partially at least, of the adoption of the Christian canonical marriage discipline. The Anglo-Normans do not encounter the excessive abuses which were complained of before their arrival. The status of women implicit in the rewritten literary texts and in the lives of the Saints at this period is no longer consistent with the almost total absence of rights found in the earliest law texts. The religious and lyrical poetry of the twelfth and thirteenth centuries implies this change in the status of women. The emancipation of women, which the long preface to the *Cain Adomnain* claims was brought about by the monk Adomnan, can be dated in the period when the first effects of the papal reform were felt. The legal change is reflected in the reinterpreting of native Irish law which began at this time.[4]

'The existence of . . . satires indicates a secure tradition. They are aimed in part at some of the practices of the twelfth century church, rather than its ideas. Asceticism was still to be pursued, in fact and not in fantasy, as in the newly founded Cistercian houses. Learning was still revered, though MacConglinne makes fun of the pedants. A reputation for hospitality, in which the great monasteries took pride, was still desirable, only the empty show is derided. Men still went to Rome or even Jerusalem on pilgrimage, but there are warnings against the devil in a man's shoes who infects him with the spirit of restlessness. Much of the old spirit remained, though alongside a new concept of organisation . . . At the same time men of learning were transcribing, compiling, glossing, and composing, in the pride of their unique heritage.'[5]

Reorganisation along diocesan and episcopal lines had taken firm root in the spirit of things before the Anglo-Normans arrived. The newcomers gave a filip to constitutional and structural reform. But from the very beginning there was the invisible barrier between the *ecclesia inter Hibernos* and the customs of the Anglo-Irish churchmen. In our terms, whereas basic conformity to an organisational discipline with dogmatic justification was acceptable, the full implications of this system as lived in medieval England or Europe was not. Among other things, whether the royal prerogatives had papal endorsement or not, Irish Christianity was never more than notionally committed to the ideas of royal assent to ecclesiastical elections, royal confirmation of candidates and royal custody of temporalities during vacancies, whether episcopal or monastic. After nearly seventy years of English and papal pressure, the chapter of Cashel in a letter to the Pope could see no reason why – either by law or custom – the royal government should have anything to do with ecclesiastical appointments.[6]

The spirit and traditions of Irish Christianity, whatever its future evolution and however its area of influence might fluctuate, remained a distinct way of life within the Christian communion in the greater part of what may have been known to the outside world as the lordship of Ireland. A different language was probably the greatest barrier against being swamped by the monolithic medieval Church. The English failed to penetrate for lack of clergy who spoke the native tongue. The Popes were frustrated by the same problem when they attempted to provide neutral continental bishops as a solution to 'the continuous war between Irish and English' over ecclesiastical appointments. At the end of the thirteenth century an Anglo-Irish bishop complained to the king that the religious in his area were preaching sedition in the Irish language.[7] The language barrier is reflected in the handwriting and calligraphy. Unlike the other local or national scripts which were superseded by the universal carolingian minuscule in the ninth to the eleventh centuries, the Irish insular minuscule reached its perfection in the twelfth century, and after the Normans came it became 'the Gaelic bookhand – a hand which, substantially unchanged, is at the bottom of modern Gaelic handwriting and printing.'[8] After the twelfth century, a distinctive language in a distinctive calligraphy are the hallmarks of the literary expression of Irish Christianity.

In the thirteenth century, to the intangible unity of common traditions and faith, was added the equally intangible sense of opposition to the impositions of English, and sometimes papal, laws and policy. It is one thing to conform – for various *ad hoc* reasons – to the organisational details of an outside tradition; it is another to believe that they are necessary. As the thirteenth century progressed, territory after territory reverted – after periods of apparent conformity – to an outlook and a mode of action that was not determined by English ecclesiastical custom or contemporary canon law. Such apparently contradictory behaviour highlights the distinctly personal and individual understanding of the Church, as well as its structural flexibility. It is an attitude expressed by St Columbanus whose verbal assertions of loyalty to the See of Peter as the guide and teacher of truth accompany a hope that the Pope will not expect blind conformity in disciplinary matters and social expression. It occurs too in Eriugena whose view that authority proceeds from right reasons and never reason from authority underlines an understanding of things that could ignore alien disciplinary decrees – papal, royal or episcopal – with equanimity.

Common opposition to Anglo-papal impositions accentuated the sense of otherness which had been apparent since the tenth century.[9] While this development intensified the knowledge of Christian belief among the semi-pagan Irish (whose existence in the twelfth century horrified Giraldus Cambrensis), Irish Christianity, already identified with native culture, became more conscious of a separate identity. This was not nationalism in the modern sense but it was a bulwark against the impositions of a centralisation from abroad. Significantly, a poem of this period – foisted on the sixth century Columcille of Iona – embodies the phrase: 'if I die, it shall be from the excess of the love I have for the Gael.'[10]

In the religious literature of the post-invasion period 'God was regarded as an Irish ruler to whom the poet had certain duties and from whom he expected certain rewards. The poet might approach God directly, but in case of any little difficulty he had recourse to God's mother, or – failing her – to any saint that he thought might be sufficiently influential.'[11]

God I ask for two things only
    Heaven when my life is done
Payment as befits a poet –
    for my poem pay a son

Plead with Him O Mother Mary
    Let Him grant the child I crave
Womb that spun God's human tissue
    I no human issue leave.

Brigid after whom they named me
Beg a son for my reward
Let no poet empty-handed
Leave the dwelling of his lord.[12]

And when it was rumoured that a papal condemnation of professional poetry had been issued, the reaction was:

The Son of Mary will give me a reward that no human being could give me; for one of my excellent poems I shall get Heaven as O'Heffernan got it. All praise of men is praise of Him who created them all; no man on earth has any praise that is not also praise of His wonder.[13]

In these religious poems 'son or wife or brother was commemorated in death as part of a system of which the king was the earthly and God the heavenly head. God, whose man the poet is, has deprived him of one of his privileges, and as a loyal servant the poet must accept this, but always the complaint is against the king, not against life itself.

It was the king of hosts and roads
Who snatched her from me in her prime;
Little she wished to leave alone
The man she loved before her time.

Life itself never seems to become detached in their minds from its individual and slightly peculiar Author.[14]

There is something too in the attitude of the poets

which seems to reflect the churchmen's apparently ready tolerance of the Normans. 'When Geoffrey O'Daly' a century and a half after our period, 'explains to the earl of Desmond that there are two sorts of poetry, one intended for the Irish, the other for the English, and says "You need take no notice of this, it is our custom", he is not being cynical. Upsetting it might be, but not cynical.'[15] In ecclesiastical affairs the same mind could readily adapt to the curiosities of imported procedures without in any way accepting the postulates which underlay the alien customs.

Irish churchmen were to find out rather quickly that the canon law and medieval procedure were not nearly so rigid or monolithic as the intermediate interpreters in England and Dublin would lead them to believe. They probably never became as adept at manipulating the law for their own ends as their Anglo-Irish rivals, but by not overestimating the importance of any human law in the Christian life they remained to a considerable extent immune from the worst effects of ecclesiastical politics and legal aggression. Besides, the native Irish ecclesiastical tradition had had fairly close organisational contacts with the papacy before the Anglo-Normans arrived. An Irish king, possibly Donnchadh Ua Cearbhaill *ri Oirghialla*, received a warm letter – *te sicut catholicum principem et christianissimum regem* (a title, soon, in the Irish context, to be taken over by the king of England) – from Pope Alexander III thanking him for his kindness to a papal envoy. The envoy had come to announce the council of Tours in 1162 and, by all appearances, he had reported favourably to Rome about the Irish Christian tradition.

On this occasion, the Pope readily granted the requests of both the Irish king and the abbot of Mellifont whom he had commended.

In this connection it is important to note that the coming of the Normans did not lead to a sudden catastrophic change in Irish life. For the second half of the twelfth century a number of new historical sources are available – largely as a result of Norman administrative practice. A regular series of English writs and royal correspondence concerning Ireland begins in 1172. Papal documents appear in large numbers. Monastic and episcopal charters and hosts of other private documents and letters are extant from this period also. Most of these Latin documents have been calendared in English summaries. Writers have tended to work with this new type of evidence to the exclusion of the continuing evidence in the native sources. More important, a tendency has developed to interpret the native Irish sources in the light of the more accessible and more easily read evidence in the translated Latin sources. Frequently Latin documents present the point of view of an alien and uncomprehending mind. Indeed, it is quite clear that the Latin language was quite unable to express the concrete ideas or cope with the reasoning of the Irish mind.

While the foreign sources begin with the coming of the Normans and perhaps leave a superficial impression that a new era had opened up in the history of Christianity in the country, the native evidence suggests no such break in continuity. The spirit and content of the annalistic entries continues in the same vein without a break, before, during and after the years of the invasion. The new 'foreigners' are often mentioned after 1169, but little of special significance is attached to their presence. After a time, the 'foreigners' of the moment will be absorbed, and then the term will be attributable to the next generation of colonists. The English king gets little mention – highlighting the fact that he did not rule Ireland in an active sense, but rather allowed the stalemate between Anglo-Irish and Gael to evolve on its own momentum.

The continuity in native tradition is seen too in religious architecture. The renaissance which began early in the century with Cormac's chapel at Cashel and in Glendalough, gathered momentum throughout the twelfth century with such fine cathedrals and abbeys as Clonfert, Killaloe, Ardfert, Tuam, Clonmacnoise, Killeshin, Rahan, Dysert O'Dea, Kilmakkedar, and Inchagoill on the Corrib. The tradition was still flourishing, if somewhat refined by outside influences, in the early decades of the thirteenth century when the abbeys and churches of Boyle, Ballintubber, Cong, Corcomroe, Inishmaine, Knockmoy and others were constructed in the areas still under native rulers.

After the synod of Kells in 1152 the emphasis in the Irish Church was still organisational, concerned with the establishment and growth of some form of episcopal-diocesan system. But there are two aspects to this develop ment. By 1152 there was a broad consensus of opinion that the establishment of the hierarchy was demanded for the good of religion. It was the common practice all over the world, it was being encouraged and insisted upon by the *comarba* (successor) of Peter in Rome, and it had a dogmatic basis. The high-king had strongly supported the scheme since the first Irish diocese had been founded in Dublin with papal approval early in the eleventh century. Gradually the idea of the importance of bishops developed and grew in the different ecclesiastical principalities. In some places the hereditary church ruler was induced to accept episcopal orders, notably in Armagh in 1106, in others, new bishops – often with the assistance of a local king, e.g. Donnchadh O Cearbhaill in Clogher – set themselves up in business in opposition to the ruling church family. What was happening was that one set of ecclesiastics or churchmen were ousting another set of churchmen. This fact bacomes more clear under the second aspect of the canonical reform. There never was a consensus as to the social and economic implications of the changeover to episcopal government. There is no evidence that the reformers had any serious blueprint whereby they would adapt the episcopal system to Irish conditions, much less that they intended to adopt the political, social and economic implications of the diocesan system in England or the continent of Europe. The hierarchical scheme drawn up by Bishop Gilbert of Limerick early in the twelfth century is devoid of economic details and shows little evidence of Pseudo-Isidorian influence. And nearly all the evidence demonstrates that the native environment would radically modify any imported notion of how episcopal government should work. The evidence of later centuries shows that in many areas bishops established their dioceses afresh, and left the traditional ecclesiastical families their social prestige and their property. Perhaps the most common evolution of the diocesan bishoprics involved a compromise with the old system, and however dubious the rigid canonists, then and now, might view this development, the concepts of blood relationship and of local family prestige of a traditional ecclesiastical nature played an important role in the history of Irish Christianity until the nineteenth century.

Nor must the reform movement be seen simply in terms of the imposition of a right canonical discipline on an outmoded and wrong ecclesiastical organisation. This again is to lose historical perspective or to view the situation through Norman or continental eyes. The old system embodied a genuine faith and its monastic structure continued to flourish in the eleventh and twelfth centuries. We have much more than Giraldus Cambrensis' word for this. Very many of the old communities rather easily adopted the religious rules introduced from outside, while the new foundations were not short of novices. No genuine history of Irish monasticism at this period has yet been written, but it is clear that numerous centres of the coenobitical life were founded in the twelfth and thirteenth centuries on land granted by Irish kings and chieftains. The connection between the Irish Benedictine congregations in Germany and Austria and the homeland during this period makes plain an unbroken Irish Christian tradition all through the years of the Norman invasion.[16] The evidence for the history of monks, canons and friars in Anglo-Irish controlled territory is more accessible, but the facts are that the sister-houses of these monasteries, priories and friaries over a great part of the country were absorbed into the Irish system. This development gave rise to the English attempts to exclude native and Irish speaking candidates from entering some religious houses, and to the splitting up of the religious congregations into two kinds of houses, Irish and Anglo-Irish, as the Cisterican Visitator found already in 1227. The monastic tradition, with its close grass roots ties, continued to play a major role, both as a religious phenomenon in itself, and as an influencing factor in the development of the diocesan bishoprics. Although the apostolic authority of the bishops was never challenged – in the theological sense – the history of Irish Christianity after the Norman invasion involves much more than the history of the bishops, particularly if an irrelevant emphasis is placed on the importance of the *consuetudines ecclesiae Anglicanae* or the details of canonical requirements. For the story of Irish Christianity in the post-Norman centuries, the history of the hierarchy's relations with the English government – or with the papacy in non-doctrinal affairs for that matter – could be a particularly misleading and largely futile exercise. At the end of the thirteenth century, for example, the Anglo-Irish bishop who complained to the king that the religious in his diocese, using the Irish language, were preaching sedition, highlights the vigour of the native Christian traditions in his area.

Irish Christianity in the medieval period cannot be understood in terms which it did not itself recognise or regard as particularly important. One of the thorniest issues in medieval Christendom outside this island concerned the relationship between the two sovereignties, the temporal and the spiritual. For the *ecclesia inter Hibernos* it never was an issue, neither before nor after the Norman invasion. One of the great problems for the medieval Church simply passed it by. And the reason is fairly clear. Behind the Church-State question is a preoccupation with abstract philosophical notions and a monolithic view of society and of the visible Church itself. The traditional Irish Christian understanding shows no interest in abstract speculation and for it the Church was much more an extension of native society, more a unity of faith and teaching, than a corporation. Contemporary European and English notions concerning the relationship between *Sacerdotium* and *Regnum* do not therefore apply in any assessment of the evolution of Irish Christianity at this period. The Annals and literature in the Irish language show a complete unawareness of the problem.

There are indications that for a long time to come episcopal government would not necessarily be equated with the continental notion of a diocese. Prior to 1152, the old Columban *paruchia* with its title to far-flung traditional jurisdiction in both Ulster and Leinster had already been reasserting itself. This renewed vigour was not only a challenge to Armagh hegemony, it was a serious modification of the canonical idea of a diocese. Furthermore, it was endorsed by an Irish reforming synod. The Annals tell us that in 1158 'a synod of the clergy of Ireland was convened at Brí milic Taidg, in Laoghaire, where there were present twenty-five bishops, with the legate of the *comarba* (successor) of Peter, to ordain rules and good morals. It was on this occasion that the clergy of Ireland, with the *comarba* of Patrick, ordered a chair, like every other bishop, for the *comarba* of Columcille, Flaithbhertach O Brolchain and the arch-abbacy of the churches of Columcille in Ireland in general.'[17] In 1161, the same Annals tell of 'a synod of the laity and clergy of Ireland' held at Dervor in Meath, where 'the churches of Columcille in Meath and Leinster were freed by the successor of Columcille, Flaithbhertach O Brolchain, and their tributes and jurisdictions were given to him for they had previously been enslaved. The visitation of Ossory was made by Flaithbhertach and the tribute due to him was seven score oxen but he selected, as a substitute for these, four hundred and twenty ounces of pure silver.'[18] Until Flaithbhertach's death in 1175 and afterwards, this traditional ecclesiastical principality, whose boundaries were more tribal than geographical and whose overlord was a bishop, continued to flourish as a real element in the movement towards reorganisation and reform.

The death of Gregory, archbishop of Dublin, in 1161, led to the appointment of Laurence O'Toole, until then abbot of Glendalough. St Laurence was a key figure in the events surrounding the Norman invasion. A man of great integrity and holiness, he is the only Irish person ever to have been canonised by the Church after due canonical process. The *Vitae* of Laurence are largely exaggerated compilations of legends and the miraculous, and they tell us little about the major events through which he lived. Yet we know that in his time he was the principal churchman in the country. Under him, for the first and last time until the seventeenth century, we find a united Irish hierarchy. The role of statesman was thrust upon him, and although he had the active support of the archbishop of the West, he failed to unite the country. It was his hope to rally the country behind the high-king,

Ruaidhri O Conchubhair, and so present what might appear like a common front to the English king. But it proved impossible to conceal that the high-king had little effective overall political control. Many of the Irish kings and chieftains saw greater and more immediate advantage in coming to terms with Henry II. Hence the failure of the treaty of Windsor.

Yet for the Church, cooperation with the English king seemed more hopeful. The synod of Cashel in 1172, convened by Henry II, was attended by the three archbishops of Dublin, Cashel and Tuam and by most of the *comarba*-bishops and important abbots from the four provinces. Giraldus Cambrensis inserted his own summary of the principal decrees of the council in his *Expugnatio Hibernica*.[19]

THE COUNCIL OF CASHEL, 1172

It was established, in the first place, that all the faithful in Ireland should repudiate concubinage with their kindred and in-laws, and should contract legitimate marriages and remain faithful to them.

Secondly, that infants be catechised at the church doors and be baptised in the sacred fonts in baptismal churches only.

Thirdly, that all the faithful of Christ should pay tithes of animals, grain and other produces, to the church of which they are parishioners.

Fourthly, that all ecclesiastical lands and their possessions be entirely free from all lay exactions of laymen: and especially that neither *reguli* nor *comites* nor any of the chieftains of Ireland or their sons –

with their followers – shall demand food or hospitality in any ecclesiastical territory, as has been their custom, nor presume to extort these dues by violence; and that the detestable custom whereby meals and maintenance are demanded four times a year from establishments belonging to churches by neighbouring chieftains shall no longer be continued.

Fifthly, that in the case of killing committed by laymen, when it is compounded for with the slayer's kin, clerics who are equally part of his kin shall not contribute to it, since as they had nothing to do with the slaying they should have nothing to do with paying compensation.

In the sixth place, that all the faithful who are ill shall make a will with due solemnity and with their confessor and neighbours present. Having paid his debts and his servants wages, if a man has a wife and children, his moveable goods shall be divided into three parts, one for his children, the second for his lawful spouse and the third for his own obsequies (=*tertia Deo*). And if they have no legitimate children, let the goods be divided into two halfs between his wife and himself. And if his lawful spouse is dead, the goods should be equally divided between the children and himself.

In the seventh place, since proper reverence in the obsequies should be rendered to those who die after a good confession, both in the celebrating of Masses and holding of vigils and in the manner of burial, so all divine services are to be carried out in all parts of the church [in Ireland] on the model of

the most holy [universal] Church according to what
the English church observes.

This legislation summarizes fairly concisely the aims of
the Irish reform movement since the beginning of the
twelfth century. Despite the evident Anglo-Norman
presentation and discipline, the emphasis is pastoral and
concrete. Whether the reference to the customs of the
English church in the last canon was originally in the
legislation or whether it is merely Giraldus' interpretation
of what should be the new tone in Irish affairs, it plainly
heralded what was to be a criterion for a future section of
the Church in Ireland.

In the same year, the Annals tells us 'a synod of the
clergy and laity of Ireland was convened at Tuam, in the
province of Connacht, by Ruaidhri O Conchubhair and
Cadhla O Dubhthaigh, archbishop of Tuam, and three
churches were consecrated by them.'[20] Unfortunately the
Irish sources – as usual – do not supply us with the details
of the affairs dealt with at Tuam, yet this synod may have
been of greater importance for the *ecclesia inter Hibernos*
than the meeting called by Henry II at Cashel. Its
composition was more in keeping with the Irish tradition
in church councils. The fact that it was convened by the
high-king and by the archbishop of Connacht, in the same
year as Henry II's council, may well make it the first move
in the separation of the two church traditions.

Gille mac Liag, the archbishop of Armagh, did not
attend the council of Cashel due to his feebleness and
age, but on a later visit to Dublin he endorsed the decrees.
He died in 1173 and was immediately replaced by the

abbot of SS Peter and Paul at Armagh, Conchubhair mac Concoille. All that we know about this 'successor' of Patrick is that he left for Rome soon after his succession 'to confer with the successor (*comarba*) of Peter.' He died in 1175 on his way back, but his visit to Rome may have had something to do with the arrival in the north a year or so later of a papal legate, Cardinal Vivian. The already confused ecclesiastical situation in the northern province was by then further disturbed by the incursion of a Norman army under John de Courcy, and the legate had to be rescued from him by the royal government in Dublin. Cardinal Vivian's contribution to the Irish scene was to proclaim, at a council in Dublin, papal confirmation for the rights of the king of England in Ireland: in future they might invade the sanctuary of churches in Ireland with impunity whenever the Irish used this right of sanctuary to hide food from the marauding foreigners.[21] This type of policy was not calculated to endear the papacy, any more than the king of England, to native Irish churchmen.

Archbishop Laurence of Dublin became involved in the north when he returned from the Third Lateran Council in 1179 as papal legate. Under his guidance the vacancy in Armagh of 1180 was filled by the appointment of Tomaltach O Conchubhair, the nephew of the high-king Ruaidhri O Conchobhair. The appointment of a man from Connacht belonging to the kindred of O Conchubhair follows Laurence O'Toole's policy of supporting the fiction of the high-kings's overall hegemony. At about the same time, another member connected with the O Conchubhair, Felix O Ruadhain, was appointed abbot of

Saul in the north. By now the archbishop of Dublin had abandoned hope of co-operating with the king of England and was clearly working against him. These events brought the northern province face to face with the existence of a threat from an alien ecclesiastical system. When archbishop Tomaltach O Conchubhair died in 1201, the province split in two. The Anglo-Irish bishops of the two northern dioceses – for by then Norman appointees had been intruded in both Meath and Connor – sided with King John's agents in supporting the government candidate, while the Irish bishops meeting in Armagh selected and consecrated – contrary to canonical procedure and the customs of the English church it was claimed – the abbot of the Augustinian house at Bangor, Echdonn mac Giolla Uidhir. By this time the issues in the Church in Ireland were becoming clear for all to see. The legate informed the Pope that in these matters there was 'the greatest contention between the Irish and the English.'[22]

It is not surprising that no northern representative attended the Third Council of the Lateran. The eastern and western provinces were represented by their respective metropolitans and the bishops of Limerick, Lismore and Killaloe attended from the south. The small number of Irish prelates attending this Council may have something to do with the tactics of the English king. As they passed through England the bishops were constrained to accept royal instructions on how they should behave at the papal curia. While some prelates might not accept such interference and hence stay at home, Laurence O'Toole seems simply to have ignored the king's instructions – at least insofar as the king understood them. Among other documents he obtained two letters of protection from the Pope – one for his own diocese and another for the diocese of Glendalough. These letters were an affront to the king's plans, particularly the one concerning Glendalough. The Anglo-Irish attempts to suppress this diocese were certainly not supported by the Irish archbishop of Dublin.

Shortly after his return from Rome, the archbishop of Dublin convened a synod in his capacity as legate.

In the year 1170 [recte 1179] . . . there was a great convocation of the clergy at Clonfert by commission of the Pope, for the reformation of certain abuses for a long time customary in Ireland. These were the bishops and clergy that were in that assembly, viz. O'Toole archbishop of Dublin and Leinster and legate of Ireland, the bishop of Meath Echtigern mac Maoil Chiarain, Bishop O Cerbhaill of Oirghialla, Cadhla O Dubhthaigh archbishop of Connacht, Celechair O hArmedhaig, bishop of Clonfert, Tomaltach O Conchubhair bishop of Magh Ai [region of Elphin], O Maolfhoghmhair bishop of Tirawley and Tireragh on the Moy, O Ruadhain [bishop of Kilmacduagh?] the abbot of Clonmacnoise, the *comarba* of St Ciaran and the *comarba* of St Brendan etc., where it was laid down by them a constitution that no layman should have rule over any church or church matters from thenceforth; that no portion canons should be sought of women their husbands living, that holy orders should not be given to bishop or priest sons; and, for example of these their constitutions they took the livings of seven bishops that had bishoprics and were laymen.'[23]

The main theme of the council seems fairly clear, to substitute men in Holy Orders for the traditional ecclesiastical chieftains who were not. But this time, it was felt that, in some areas at least, an attempt could be made to take over the possessions of hereditary churchmen. The ruling concerning women is too obscure in the garbled translation of the last Annals of Clonmacnoise to have an obvious meaning.

The need for legislation of this kind, as late as 1179, is significant. The fabric through which the Christian faith expressed itself among the native Irish was still *sui generis,* and conformity with European or English structures was not a compelling motive. In 1190, for example, the archbishop of Cashel obtained papal approval for the ordination of sons of *pontifices* and their appointment to the parishes or churches where their fathers had served, or were still serving.[24] In 1202 the papal legate was aghast to find family succession a qualification for appointment to the archbishopric of Tuam and western dioceses generally.[25] Later evidence shows that the hereditary churchmen had no intention of handing over their possessions to the new men whose office was designed to be primarily spiritual but which now had become so closely identified with the foreigner.

Laurence O'Toole is a complex personality who, despite his profound involvement in a critical period of his country's history, has defied an adequate biographical study. His background was exclusively native Irish; he belonged to a prestigious Leinster family. He was undoubtedly a man of great sanctity and an ascetic in the traditional native sense. His devotion to the task of reform and reorganisation was total, a characteristic of his inflexibility of mind perhaps as much as a result of his dedication to the Church. He was utterly convinced of the need for some constitutional reform in the Church, but, to his dismay, he found that these new structures had suddenly been taken over by the English king. Here was a misconception his native mind simply could not deal with. According to his lights the pretensions of the temporal authorities were something alien to the very need for reform. Reform for him was the reassertion of the spiritual dimension, a dimension which had a unique imperative within it. This imperative was not capable of any dilution by temporal considerations, even ecclesiastical ones; yet, the papacy itself appeared to be endorsing the constitutional pretensions of the monarchy. The complexity of the situation as St Laurence saw it was as close as the medieval Irish mind was ever to get to formal involvement in theories on Church-State relations. Laurence ended his days at loggerheads with the king of England, who strenuously complained that Laurence had harmed the monarchy at the papal curia. One has the distinct impression that the archbishop of Dublin was only vaguely aware of what exactly the king was annoyed about, an impression which comes mainly from the repeated attempts of Laurence to gain an audience with the king of France. The pathetic story that some frustrated individual hit the archbishop on the head with a brick while he was staying with the monks at Eu in Normandy highlights an ascetic rigidity which always found it difficult to deal with some human weaknesses and the complexities of politics despite the highest and most admirable of ideals. He died in exile, shortly after the incident with the brick, in fruitless deadlock with the government.

The death of St Laurence in 1181 brought with it the end of an era. From 1181 until after the Reformation the archbishop of dublin was to be a central figure in the Anglo-Irish church and was frequently an official of the royal government as well. No native Irishman held the office after Laurence until the the seventeenth century. Outside of Dublin, the Anglo-Irish church made inroads more or less in step with English military advance. The east coast and parts of the north fell permanently under its sway although at no time in subsequent centuries is it possible to indicate the depth of commitment to the Anglo-Irish tradition in most areas. The western region remained largely under native control until well into the next century – mainly due to the existence of an independent kingdom of Connacht until 1224.

Meantime in the north, the archbishop of Armagh, despite a troubled episcopate, took advantage of the confusion to absorb a large section of the neighbouring diocese of Clogher. The transfer to Armagh of most of its present territory in the modern county Louth took place – possibly with Norman aid – in the last decade of the twelfth century, and it may have been endorsed at a synod held in Dublin in 1192.[26] At about the same time the diocese of Clogher was expanded northwestwards, and this was to cause great tension between the bishops of

Clogher and Derry in the thirteenth century, until Derry recovered its stolen lands.[27] In the other areas of the province of Armagh, where the Normans did not penetrate, the pre-Norman ecclesiastical structure remained undisturbed.

Except in the more remote areas, the southern province adapted more readily to the customs and discipline of Latin Christianity. Yet it was to this area that the initiative in the *ecclesia inter Hibernos* passed at the beginning of the thirteenth century. In 1228, the Englishman who had been appointed Cistercian Visitor, warned the government that the nerve centre of the growing Irish revolt against alien institutions was in Munster.

A Cistercian, Muirgheas O hEnna became archbishop of Cashel sometime after 1182. The Annals refer to him as 'the chief bishop of Munster.' He may have visited the papal curia after his discussions with Gerard, a cleric of the church at Rome, in 1185-86. A number of problems arising out of Irish customs were put to the Pope by him in 1190. Shortly afterwards Muirgheas O hEnna became papal legate 'of all-Ireland.' As legate he convened the synod of Dublin in 1192 and endorsed the suppression of the diocese of Glendalough. He also settled a dispute between John Comyn and the cathedral chapter of Holy Trinity, and probably attended the ceremony establishing St Patrick's cathedral. In his own province disputed episcopal successions and fierce battles between foreigner and Gaedhil were the order of the day. Munster had been carved up among numerous colonists, at least on paper, by grants of Henry II and Prince John. Yet in the south the native tradition was more organised and less isolationist. In the diocese of Ross there was a dual problem: the Irish squabbled among themselves over the family succession, and the Anglo-Irish took advantage of the dispute to install a bishop of their own. Both the bishop of Cork and Domhnall McCarthy, king of Munster, were involved. In Cork itself, by 1199 the bishop had obtained a detailed charter of confirmation and protection from the Pope.[28] In the meantime the legate's activities were hardly guided by canonical discipline. In 1195, he expelled the bishop of Killaloe and installed a member of his own family, Conchubhair O hEnna. The intruder held on to the see until his death, on the return journey from the Lateran council in 1216. In Ardfert there was a dispute in these same years which, from the information available to the Pope, was again caused principally by the archbishop of Cashel. The archbishop had refused to consecrate the bishop-elect and tried to intrude another of his personal candidates. For his part in this affair, Innocent III suspended him, but the censure had little effect in Gaelic Ireland and the archbishop carried on unworried by the theoretical change in his status. Pope Innocent gave vent to his exasperation with Irish churchmen in one letter concerning this case. 'We are staggered, and with good reason we are perturbed, that some of our brethren and fellow-bishops, whom one would expect to act like grown men, behave in a way that has nothing whatever to do with right reason, and show that they are full of audacity and presumption rather than virtue of obedience.'[29]

At the same time, the Pope was hearing loud protests from the English archbishop of Dublin who had been sent into exile by Hamo de Valognes, the justiciar.

Innocent III decided to send a special legate to look into the confused affairs of the Church out in the Atlantic.

The legate, John, cardinal priest of St Stephen *in Monte Celio*, arrived early in 1202. He first turned his attention to the disputed succession to Armagh, where the problem was complicated by rivalry between the old and more recently arrived colonists. Before leaving the north, the legate appointed a Cistercian from the abbey of Melrose in Scotland to the vacant bishopric of Down.[30] Shortly afterwards he confirmed the translation of the cathedral church of Meath from Clonard to the more amenable Newtown near Trim. Two years earlier, the Irish had attacked Clonard 'to injure the foreigners that were in it.'[31] In Dublin the legate found that the archbishop was still in exile, but that the spiritualities of the see were being administered by the archbishop of Cashel – on the instructions of the unpredictable King John. He decided to hold a synod which, the Annals inform us, was 'a synod of the clergy of Ireland both foreigner and Gael.' Then, we are told, 'a synod of Connacht, both laics and clergy, was held in Athlone, with the same cardinal at the end of a fortnight.'[32] It was probably here that the legate settled the Tuam succession dispute, when Felix O Ruadhain the prior of Saul in County Down, was appointed archbishop, and also here that he gave judgment in favour of the suppression of the diocese of Mayo. These unpopular decisions which, the legate informed the Pope, made it impossible for the new archbishop to travel to Rome for the *pallium* because of the hostility of the surrounding territory, were an added reason for the legate himself not travelling westward beyond the Shannon.

The last two decades of the twelfth century were years of intense political strife in the largely uninvaded province of Connacht. As the position of Ruaidhri O Conchubhair, the high-king whom Laurence O'Toole and Cadhla O Dubhthaigh archbishop of Connacht had fought to uphold, became weaker, the battle for hegemony in the west was fought between three family contestants, Conchubhair Maenmuighe, Cathal Carrach and Cathal Croibhdearg – with the last of these emerging as victor at the end of the century. When referring to the end of the O Conchubhair hegemony in Connacht in 1233, the Annals give us an insight, through native eyes, of this troubled period. 'This was the termination of the sovereignty of the descendants of Ruaidhri O Conchubhair, king of Eirinn: for the Pope had offered right over Eirinn to Ruaidhri and his seed after him forever, and six married wives, provided that he desisted from the sin of the women from thenceforth; but Ruaidhri did not accept this. And as he did not accept, God took kingship and sovereignty from his seed forever in punishment of the sin of the women.'[33]

Except for a brief de Courcy raid in 1187, the Normans did not penetrate deeply into the west before the end of the century. Nevertheless, shortly after this raid, an Irish bishop of a hitherto unheard of diocese, Annaghdown, appears. More strange was this man's presence at the coronation of Richard I at Westminster in 1189. Thereafter we find this bishop, Conn O Meallaigh, acting in close cooperation with the Anglo-Irish prelates and barons. Before the end of the century he founded the Premonstratensian monastery at Annaghdown and installed his son,

Thomas, as abbot. In 1242, Thomas, whose mother was a nun, was a candidate for the vacant see of Annaghdown.[34]

The trouble in Tuam which brought the legate to Athlone began when one side to the dispute charged the other with nepotism. According to his report to the Pope, the legate was scandalised to find that 'in Irish churches a detestable abuse is found, especially in the church of Tuam and other places in the west, whereby sons succeed their fathers, not only in lesser ecclesiastical positions but also even in archbishoprics and bishoprics.' It seems that Cadhla O Dubhthaigh, the archbishop who died in 1201, had consecrated his nephew so that the traditional family succession would be secure, for already a grandfather and a great grandfather had been head churchman in Tuam. The legate succeeded in having the nephew removed 'but with some difficulty.' Felix O Ruadhain, brother-in-law of one of the O Conchubhair chieftains, was appointed with the consent of the suffragans.[35] Laurence O'Toole's support for the O Conchubhair hegemony had been responsible for Felix' earlier appointment as abbot of Saul. Now as archbishop of Connacht, Felix also advocated constitutional change. Unlike Laurence however, his motives are less clear and he had no qualms about the change in direction that was taking place as a result of constitutional reform. His wholehearted adoption of Anglo-Irish policies was seen at home as a betrayal.

The charge of nepotism in Tuam may have been no more than a convenient canonical argument in the battle for western hegemony. At this time there were O Ruadhain bishops in the territory of Luighne (Achonry), Ui Fiachra Muaidhe (Killala) and Ui Fiachra Aidhne (Kilmacduagh).

But Cathal Croibhdearg O Conchubhair, the actual holder of the title 'king of Connacht' was a supporter of the O Dubhtaigh line; when he failed in Tuam, he may well have installed the disappointed nephew of Cadhla O Dubhthaigh in the diocese of Mayo, because a bishop of that name appears in Mayo shortly after this time. In Luighne too, there was a rival claimant to the O Ruadhain bishop. Felix O Ruadhain had therefore a strong personal motive for his attempt to suppress the diocese of Mayo and make it a simple parish church of Tuam. But the legate's confirmation of the suppression was premature. After an appeal to the Pope, papal judges-delegate – one of whom was the archbishop of Armagh – reversed the legate's decision. Cele O Dubhtaigh remained as bishop of Mayo until 1210. Later the legate James suppressed Mayo again, and Pope Gregory II confirmed the suppression in 1240.[36]

Although the trouble in Tuam was connected with the battle for western hegemony among the Irish, the appointment of O Ruadhain introduced a new pressure into the western province. His attempt to suppress the diocese of Mayo was in keeping with Anglo-Irish church policy. And it was to that tradition that he turned when the legate left. In 1211 he held an important synod.

'There was a great convocation of the clergy of Connacht before the bishop of Tuam to make constitutions for the taking away of termon lands or *comarba* lands, and annexing them to the bishoprics of the dioceses where they lay, where the *comarba* of St Patrick, the *comarba* of St Brendan, the *comarba* of St Ciaran and the *comarba* of St Feichin with many others appeared.'[37]

Again here we have only the garbled translation of the original source. As the text stands, the purpose of the synod appears clear enough, namely to detach their lands from the hereditary churchmen and give them to the newly established churchmen, the bishops. But we know from later evidence that a more vexed question must certainly have been in the agenda – and the compiler of the Annals of Clonmacnoise (or the translator) may have misunderstood his source. During the General Council of 1216, the archbishops of Armagh and Tuam brought a dispute over these very lands to the Pope. For Felix O Ruadhain it was a case of establishing his full rights in his own diocese and province according to the norms of the imported canon law. For his opponent, however, Felix was attempting to destroy immemorial tradition by excluding the customary rights of the successor of Patrick in the traditional *paruchia* of Patrick in the west. It is a measure of the new understanding of local Irish custom that Honorius III brought into the papal curia that the archbishop of Tuam was restricted to 'episcopal rights only' over nine churches in his own diocese, clearly leaving the ancient rights of the *comarba* of Patrick intact.[38] In 1241 the Annals tell us: 'The *comarba* of Patrick, i.e. the German (Albert Suerbeer) came to Ireland, having privileges from the Pope over the churches of Patrick in Ireland . . . Peace was made by the *comarba* of Patrick with the archbishop of Connacht, and with the other bishops likewise, on account of Patrick's land in Connacht.'[39]

But O Ruadhain paid dearly for his Anglo-Norman sympathies. Already the legate had told Innocent III that the archbishop was unable to move out of the immediate territory *propter hostilitatem terrae*, and in 1213 King John instructed his justiciar, the archbishop of Dublin, to give hospitality to Felix, at that time in exile from his diocese.[40] In 1216, the Annals tell us: 'the archbishop O Ruadhain was cruelly and violently taken prisoner by the Connacht-men and Maelisa O Conchobhair, and put in chains, a thing that we never heard of before, viz. an archbishop being manacled.'[41]

Felix O Ruadhain attended the Fourth Lateran Council in 1216, and while in Rome gave evidence in favour of the suppression of the Irish diocese of Glendalough.

John Papiron, legate of the Roman church, when he came to Ireland, found Dublin with a bishop who then exercised the episcopal office within the walls. In the same diocese he found another church in the mountains, which likewise was called a city and had a certain *co-episcopus*. Delivering the *pallium* to the bishop then ruling the church of Dublin, the legate constituted the excellent city of Dublin to be metropolis of that province and directed that the diocese containing both cities should be divided so that a part should remain to the church in the mountains, intending, as we firmly believe, that on the death of him that then presided over that church, this part should revert to the metropolis, and he would have effected this at the time if the insolence of the Irish who then had power in that land had not deferred it. When Henry, king of England, heard of this intention from several persons, adhering to the action and will of the legate he granted that other portion to the metropolis. In like manner John, now king of England, after he had heard great men and elders in the land, granted it to John, predecessor of the present archbishop. Furthermore, that holy church in the mountains was held in great reverence from early times on account of St Kevin who lived there as a hermit. But now it is so deserted and desolate for almost forty years that from a church it has become a den of thieves and a pit of robbers, so that by reason of the deserted and naked wilderness there are more homicides committed in that valley than in any other part of Ireland.'[42]

This piece of Pseudo-Isidorian justification in the mouth of Felix O Ruadhain indicates another complex Irish ecclesiastic whose life as a churchman so markedly differs from that of Laurence O'Toole. The concluding paragraph of his testimony in favour of the suppression of the diocese of Glendalough shows another motive for adopting constitutional change. By this time the fire had gone out of the native spiritual revival and none would consider this archbishop of Connacht a reformer. But he too seems to have been out of tune with his time, and although he lingered on into a ripe old age, he appears to have spent most of his years under the protection of the government and out of the reach of his outraged people in the west. Despite his wholehearted adoption of their ways, Felix O Ruadhain seemed curiously paralysed when it came to benefiting for himself in the world of Anglo-Irish ecclesiastical politics.

It can hardly be overstressed that the Irish understanding of the visible Church, including the successor of Peter at its head, was far less corporate and hence less organisationally uniform than any important idea. The ecclesiastical structure was understood, and would continue to be understood, in terms of Irish law and social tradition. The use of such terms as episcopal government, diocese, election and ecclesiastical office could therefore be misleading if they are understood solely in a conventional sense. The Annals are the most accurate reflection of the ecclesiastical realities. Bishops are consistently referred to by the old titles. The metropolitan of the west is more usually referred to as the archbishop of Connacht – a fluctuating territorial entity with little political significance. The bishops have titles such as Comnaicne, Luighne, Sil Muiredaigh, Ui Fiachra, Tir Eoghain and Tir Conaill, instead of Ardagh, Achonry, Elphin, Killala, Derry and Raphoe – and most of them still worked with traditional rather than imported instruments. In Killala, out of the six *comarba*-bishops between 1140 and 1230, four of them were from the O Maolfoghmhair family, yet a papal confirmation of property and rights had been obtained from Innocent III. Of the six *comarba*-bishops in Tir Eoghain between 1152 and 1293, two were of the O Cubhtaigh family and four of the O Cearbhaillain family.

The papal confirmation for Killala was granted at about the same time as a number of papal letters were sent to King Cathal Croibhdearg.[43] From Innocent III the king of Connacht got recognition for rights similar to those claimed by the king of England, e.g. the right to give the royal assent to elections – although someone advised the Pope to warn him not to abuse this privilege. Cathal also asked clarification about the rights of sanctuary and ecclesiastical immunity. But it is clear that these rights were sought with an eye to Cathal's position in the eyes of the English king: they could not be taken seriously in the west where Cathal Croibhdearg's influence would come from his family connections and whatever physical pressure he could exert.

In the north, the *paruchia* of St Columcille was an active ecclesiastical reality in the first two decades of the thirteenth century. In 1203 the Annals record that 'Domhnall Ua Brolchain prior [of Iona] noble senior noted for his intelligence, for form, for appearance, for disposition, for gentleness, for magnanimity, for benevolence, for piety, for wisdom, entered the way of the flesh, after great suffering and most excellent penance on 27 April.' Then the following year the same source notes that 'a monastery was built by Cellach [abbot of Iona] in the centre of the enclosure of Iona, without any right, in dishonour of the community of Iona, so that he did great damage to the place. A hosting, however, was made by the clergy of Ireland, namely by Florence O Cearbhaillain bishop of Tir Eoghain and by Meal Isu O Dorig, that is bishop of Tir Conaill, and by the abbot of the monastery of SS Peter and Paul in Armagh and by Amalgaidh O Fergail abbot of the monastery of Derry and by Ainmire O Cobhthaigh and a large number of the community of Derry and a large number of the clergy of the north, so that they razed the monastery according to the law of the Church. The aforesaid Amalgaidh assumed the abbacy of

Iona by the choice of the foreigners and the Gael.'[44]

In 1214 we are told that 'Thomas, son of Uchtrach and Ruaidhri, son of Ragnall, plundered Derry completely and took the treasures of the community of Derry, and of the north of Ireland as well, from within the church of the monastery. Ua Cathair and the men of Craibh came to Derry to seize a house in which the sons of Mac Lochlainn were, and they killed the chief cellarer of the monastery of Derry who was among them. But God and St Columcille wrought a great miracle there: the man that assembed and mustered the force, namely Mathgamain Mac Aithne, was immediately killed in reparation for the affront to Columcille at the door of Columcille's oratory. Ainmire O Cobhthaigh, abbot of the monastery of Derry, a noble cleric of outstanding piety, of gentleness, of meekness, of magnanimity, of benevolence, of great alms-giving, of wisdom and of every other good quality, *post optimam pentitentiam ingressus est viam universae carnis* in Columcille's oratory.'[45] In 1219, 'Mael Isu O Daighri *airchinneach* of Derry of Columcille – for forty years he was *airchinneach* – having done every good deed among churchmen and laity *in bono fine quievit in pace* on Sunday 8 December.' The following year 'Fonachtan Ua Bronain *comarba* of Columcille *in pace quievit*: and there occurred a dispute between the community of Derry and the Cinel Eoghain over the choice of a successor. What happened then [is this]: the community of Derry chose Mac Cathmail into the position of *comarba*, while Aedh O Neill and the Cinel Eoghain chose Flann O Brolchain. There ensued a contest between the community of Derry and O Brolchain, and O Brolchain was expelled from the *comarba*-ship. Thereafter the community of Derry and the Cinel Eoghain chose Muirchertach Ua Millugain, that is the lector (*fearleighinn*) of Derry to the *comarba*-ship, and he held the lectorship and the *comarba*-ship for a year or a little more. A dispute occurred between Geoffrey Ua Daighri, i.e. the *airchinneach* and Ua Millugain, i.e. the *comarba*, concerning the lectorship, and they sought the judgment of the *comarba* of Patrick and he made peace between them and Eoin the son of the lector was chosen for the lectorship by the judgment of the *comarba* of Patrick and the comarba of Columcille and the community of Derry.'[46]

The substance of Irish Catholicism at this period often finds expression in the records of deaths. The merit of a good life is a frequent theme. In 1207 'Mael-Petair Ua Calmain, successor of St Canice, tower of piety and hospitality of the north of Ireland rested in peace. In the words of the poet:

> *From the time of the virginal Canice*
> *Until Ua Calmain rose above the altar,*
> *It is unknown if as good saw the heavenly kingdom,*
> *Never was a monk's habit put on one so good.*
>
> *He was a master scribe of beautiful execution,*
> *Well used he keep the good rule,*
> *He practised good works on every occasion,*
> *He was a distinguished and eminent wise man.*

Although no one under heaven
Though he be made holy and without blemish
Could free the penitentiary from demons,
Still, the body of Ua Calmain could free it. [47]

On the other hand, the justice of God is the theme of a typical *obit* of an English plunderer. 'William Burke took the spoils of all the churches of Connacht, viz. Clonmacnoise, Clonfert, Millick, Kilbryan, the churches of Ui Fiachragh, Tuam, Killenen, Kilmaine, Mayo of the English, Cong of St Feichin, the abbey of Boyle, Elphin, Uaran, Roscommon with many other churches. God and the patrons of these churches showed their miracles upon him that his entrails . . . fell out of him and trailed after him to the very earth, whereof he died, impenitently without absolution or extreme unction or good burial in any church in the kingdom.' [48]

While there was little coordinated resistance to the impositions of the foreigner in the ecclesiastical fields, what there was came mostly out of the southern province of Munster. The archbishop of Cashel, the metropolitan of the province, made a determined effort to stop the worst legal aggression by journeying to see the Pope in 1219 and enlisting his aid. The archbishop's attitude anticipated by a century what the poet had to say of Munster:

Eternal God
there are two in Munster
who destroy us and what is ours.
These are the Earl of Ormond

125

and the Earl of Desmond
and those who follow them,
whom in the end the Lord will destroy
through Christ, our Lord. Amen.[49]

The archbishop's efforts were not entirely in vain. The Anglo-Norman archbishop of Dublin was quickly removed from the office of papal legate. The new legate *a latere* was instructed to put an end to certain 'detestable and vicious' legal customs. It seems that were an Englishman to charge an Irishman with theft and was supported in this charge by the word of six other Englishmen, the native was forced to make restitution despite the fact that he was innocent of the crime, that his reputation was excellent and that he could produce thirty and more witnesses to swear to his innocence; on the other hand, were an Englishman to be charged with theft from a native and were it known that he had in fact committed the crime, he could be declared innocent and freed by the simple procedure of swearing to his own innocence.[50] Discrimination of this nature by the authorities was widespread. In August 1220 and again in April 1224 Pope Honorius III condemned the unheard of temerity of the English in excluding all Irishmen, however saintly and eminent, from promotion within the Church.[51] It was surely the Anglo-Normans, and not the native Irish, who had to be commanded by the Pope to continue to recognise the archbishop of Cashel after the latter had taken on the Cistercian habit during a period of grave illness.[52]

The Popes may not have been addressing themselves any longer to Irish *reges christianissimi* as they had been before the Anglo-Normans arrived; nevertheless native Irish prelates were now finding a growing awareness at the papal curia of the differences between the *Anglici* and the *Hibernici*. Nor was it only at the papal curia that the *Hibernici*, after a period of relative isolation from active participation in continental affairs, were known to be a different race of people. An Italian at the University of Paris kept notes of his observations of the different peoples he met there. The Irish students, he noted, were commendable in their diligence during their weekday studies. In this they were outstanding. More the pity then that they drank so much alcohol at the weekends because this gave them the reputation of being the most boisterous of all the different *nationes* in Paris.

Despite the scattered nature of the entries in the Irish Annals, and the local wars and tensions which these report, a vigorous faith is evident. In 1221 'Diarmaid O Culechain, a professor of history and writing, died, i.e. a man who had more writings and knowledge than anyone that came in his own time; and it was he that wrote the Mass Book of Knock, and another Mass Book equal to it for Diarmaid Mac Oirechtaigh, his tutor, and for Gillapatraic, his foster-brother – the successors of Achadh-Fobhair (Aghagower, County Mayo) in succession.' And three years later we read 'Muirgheas Cananach, son of Ruaidhri O Conchubhair, the most expert man that ever came of the Gaedhail in reading, and in psalm-singing, and in verse-making, died this year, and was interred in Cong of Feichin, after the triumph of unction and penitence.'[53] The Mass[54] and Mary, alms-giving and the victory over death of 'repentance and unction' – as well as the 'miraculous' interventions of God and patron saints – these are the recurring concrete expressions of the Christian faith and hope in the Irish sources from the eighth century to the sixteenth.

The death of Cathal Croibhdearg O Conchubhair in 1224 brought with it the end of the independent Irish kingdom of Connacht. Before his death the colonists had already made deep inroads into the western province, and now a further victory was in sight. Yet the collapse of this tenuously organised Irish stronghold had little or no immediate effect on the native Irish Christian tradition. The *obit* of the last king of Connacht is, nevertheless, a suitable contemporary summary of a Christian attitude of mind which finds no adequate expression in a code of laws or socio-political theory.

Cathal Croibhdearg O Conchubhair, king of Connacht, and king of the Gaedhil of Ireland according to merit, died in the monastery of Knockmoy on the fifth of the kalends of June. The best Gaedhil since Brian Boromha for nobleness and for honour: the fortunate and powerful upholder of his people; rich, well-disposed and excellent maintainer of peace. It seems that in his time tithes were legally paid for the first time in Ireland. He was a fitting, pious and right-judging supporter of the Faith and Christianity; he was the punisher of the guilty and outlaws; he destroyed robbers and evil-doers; he maintained righteous laws with many victories in battle. To him God gave a good honour on earth and a heavenly kingdom beyond. He died in the habit of a monk after winning victory over the world and the devil.[55]

6

UNDERSTANDING THE PAST

'The lamentable condition of the Irish Church by the fourteenth century . . . meant that the *ecclesia hibernica* had neither constitutional nor any other sort of unity.' This conclusion by a distinguished English historian in a recent work [1] would seem to call for a bold assertion that the Irish Church had disappeared by the fourteenth century. Yet we know that it did not cease to exist at this time. However one defines its unity, we know that an Irish ecclesial reality, as opposed to a mere constitutional Church, retained the confessional allegiance of most of the people right through the upheavals of the sixteenth and seventeenth centuries. Historical perspective alone ultimately confirms the divergent paths of the two Christian expressions in post-invasion Ireland, but the contemporary evidence for the beginnings of this divergence is ample in itself.

Every expression of social unity depends, in the ultimate analysis, on a meeting of minds, and no apparent unity has a great life expectancy without a common ideology, however temporary. The unity that is expressed in the term Christian Church cannot, at any time, be understood unless account be taken of its unifying principle or ideology. The ideology in this case is faith. The Christian Church is a believing people. A believing people is rarely, if ever, physically identifiable in every respect with a corporate community – for all that a physical expression of the common submission of belief is an absolute requirement in a believing people.

There are various headings under which one might describe the manifest Christian unity which temporarily bound the recognisable forces at work in Ireland after the coming of the Normans – common creed, common symbolism, common head (however differently understood), common prayer, common written sources. With equal facility one could devise a list of headings under which these forces were recognisably divergent; it is with some of these as they manifest themselves in the behaviour of the different groups of inhabitants during the post-invasion decades that these pages have been written.

The Christian Church lays claim to a universal relevance – in accordance with the mandate 'to all men' of its founder. It also lays claim, in varying degrees, to universal allegiance. At possibly no other time, except perhaps in the first hundred years of its existence, were the terms of external allegiance being more comprehensively spelt out than in the twelfth century. But to the particularism of the individual and his local community was added, at this time, the powerful particularism of evolving nations. England was part and parcel of the mainstream constitutional developments of Europe, and its national monarchy was already struggling for the constitutional allegiance of the inhabitants of Britain against the universal constitutional claims of the Church as represented by the papacy especially. Indeed, it is in the guise of constitutional opponents that the English crown and the papacy were very often seen by the constituents of the *ecclesia inter Hibernos.*

The constitutional reorganisation which had been maintained in a strong spirit of renewal for the first seventy years of twelfth century Ireland, was immediately taken over by the Anglo-Norman authorities when the king arrived in 1172. To a large extent the structural and constitutional aspects of the reform became identified with the foreigner. The already distinct sense of otherness among the Irish, now pushed by the united Anglo-Norman expansion into a strong feeling of national difference, could only express itself in those concrete expressions of both native culture and Christianity which were little identified with a constitutional structure. Likewise, when the Anglo-Normans had to be faced on their own grounds, it was largely with the help of the papacy that the *ecclesia inter Hibernos* disputed constitutional and organisational issues with the foreigner.

For the believing Christian there is a Divine guarantee in the objective expression of belief, whatever darkness of understanding may obscure the putting into effect of this expression. In medieval Ireland, a community, a believing people, retained its identity after the coming of the Normans in ever-growing opposition to the constitutional structure that was meant to organise and represent it. The undoubtedly victorious political forces during and after the invasion succeeded merely in hiving-off an empty shell from that community. At grass-roots level, where alone

the Christian Church has ultimate relevance, the constitutional Church had little spiritual relevance and, when
the test came, hardly any community allegiance at all.

APPENDIX I

Pontificia Hibernica
Addendum
4a

To a king of the Irish. Pope Alexander III commends him for his devotion to the Apostolic See and for his reception of the papal envoy sent to convene a council (at Tours 1162). He grants the requests of the king and also of the abbot of Mellifont whom the king had commended to the Pope.

[1163-1165]

Vatican, Codex Reg. Lat. 179 fol. 152r-v
Historiae Francorum scriptores IV ed. Du Chesne, A. (Paris 1641) 657AB No. CCLIV - Falkenstein, L. 'Ein Vergessener Brief Alexanders III an einen "Rex Hibernorum"', *Archivium Historiae Pontificiae* 10 (1972) 148.

. . . illustri Hibernorum regi.[1]

Litteris sublimitatis tuae debita benignitate susceptis fidem et devotionem, quam te sicut catholicum principem et christianissimum regem circa beatum Petrum et nos ipsos firmiter exhibere cognovimus, gratam admodum acceptamque tenemus tuamque super hoc celsitudinem dignis in Domino laudibus commendamus, uberrimas serenitati tuae gratias exsolventes, quod dilectum filium.[2] Subdiaconum nostrum olim ad partes illas pro vocatione concilii destinatum regia curasti benignitate recipere et, sicut te et ipsum decuit, propensius honorare. Unde nos consideratione tuae fidei ac puritatis inducti in ea sumus voluntate ac proposito stabilitati, ut iustas petitiones tuas clementer velimus semper admittere et in his, quae cum Deo poterimus, honori et gloriae tuae celsitudinis aspirare. Ad praesens autem excellentiae tuae volumus innotescat, quod dilectum filium nostrum abbatem . . . Mellifontis, quem tua nobis serenitas commendavit, benigne recepimus et eum in iustis petitionibus suis efficaciter curavimus exaudire. Rogamus itaque magnificentiam tuam et exhort-amur in Domino quatenus in unitate catholica et devotione matris tuae sacrosanctae Romanae ecclesiae ac nostra firmus et immobilis perseveres, ut inde et premium possis eternae retributionis accipere et gratiam apostolicae sedis ac nostram pleniorem omni tempore debeas obtinere.

Appendix II

The Origins of the Primacy Controversy

Archbishop Peter Talbot put the question of ecclesiastical primacy in Ireland in its modern context some three hundred years ago. 'What, I ask, is the Primacy of Ireland? An empty title, a barren dignity, which carries with it nothing save lawsuits, strifes, dangers and odium? Moreover, should bishops be so inclined for battle, that they would not be afraid to strive with great zeal, for the empty shadow of dignity? Of what importance is it to the salvation of souls, whether the archbishop of Armagh carries off the palm and primacy, before the archbishop of Dublin, or on the other hand, Dublin takes it from Armagh?'[1]

Among the inevitable misunderstandings and controversies over precedence and jurisdiction which are strewn along the history of the Church, the disputes over primatial status have never had much more than peripheral importance. Despite a vast amount of sometimes impassioned energy devoted by interested parties to the right to use the title, primates in the western Church never became the ordinary vehicles of jurisdiction or authority. It was at the time of the Norman invasion that the idea of a primate was brought into Ireland although the battle for hegemony preceded the coming of the title of primate by a long time.

There is little firm evidence remaining for the type of ecclesiastical organisation which existed in the first century of Irish Christianity. By the sixth century, the so-called monastic Church had begun to take shape. Under this system ecclesiastical principalities or *paruchia* came into being, and a race for precedence or overlordship developed among them. The earliest claim for ecclesiastical hegemony was made by the 'metropolitan church' of Kildare, where the 'archbishop of the Irish bishops' ruled; the attitude of the *paruchia* of Columcille, if it did not claim an overall hegemony, certainly did not submit to the lordship of anyone else. But none of these early attempts was as successful as the later ambitions of the Armagh chieftains.[2] The Armagh claim was aided by political events and by the invention of a legend. 'The growth of the Patrick legend, on which the claim of Armagh to primacy was based, is closely associated with the spread of another legend, that of the "immemorial high-kingship" at Tara on which the Ui Neill monarchs grounded their claim to hegemony over the provincial kings.'[3] In the seventh century, the Armagh lawyers worked out the terms of their claim. Suzerainty was asserted over the whole of Ireland, except perhaps over that part of Leinster which was embraced by the *paruchia* of St Bridget. There were rivals, of course, acknowledged by the writers, such as Clonmacnoise, Ardstraw and Iona.[4] Nevertheless by continuous political pressure and by carefully fostering the legends concerning Patrick and the church at Armagh, the northern ecclesiastical chieftains succeeded in asserting a hegemony over most of the country. By the tenth century, when succession 'to Patrick' and to many of the monastic founders had become hereditary, laws in the name of Patrick, applicable to the entire island, had been successfully proclaimed by the *comarbai* at Armagh and taxes were collected by them during their swing through much of the country on visitation, known as the *cuairt*. As late as 1005, when the new high-king from the south, Brian Boroime, visited the north to assert his kingly claims, he acknowledged the pre-eminent position of Armagh by a gift laid on 'Patrick's altar'. It was probably at this time that he allowed a confirmation of the privileges of the clergy of Armagh to be entered in the *Liber Angeli* – the textbook of the 'imaginary claims' of the *comarbai* of Patrick.

St Patrick when going to heaven, ordered that the whole fruit of his labour, as well of baptism and of causes as of alms, should be paid to the apostolic city (*urbs*) which in Irish is named Ardd-Macha. So I have found in the books of the Irish. I, namely Mael Suthain, have written in the presence of Brian, emperor of the Irish, and what I have written he has determined for all the kings of Cashel.[5]

To transfer this kind of hegemony over a group of largely hereditary principalities to a position of primacy in the developing episcopal-diocesan system was not simply a matter of changing a name in a new environment. The episcopal system cut the ground from under the feet of any hereditary ecclesiastical chieftain. Likewise, the new system had no place in it for the type of privilege or precedence so far claimed by the men of Armagh, nor did it recognise the same *raison d'etre* for giving one bishopric jurisdiction over another. To make matters even more difficult for the 'successors of Patrick', Armagh – precisely because of its hegemony under the old system – was one of the last major centres to come to terms with the new episcopal-diocesan organisation. In fact the old Armagh hegemony came to an end with the introduction of the diocesan system; the celebrated lists of the 'successors of Patrick' all end in the twelfth century.

The concept of provincial primate was itself based on a continental invention. It appears officially for the first time in the False Decretals of the Pseudo-Isidore. His ingenious selection of early documents was calculated to demonstrate, among other things, that from early times primates had held superior jurisdiction. The 'primates' were the bishops of the most important cities, hence the frequent appeals in continental primacy disputes to the *Notitia Galliarum*. At no time, however, even when the False Decretals were thought to be more than they are, was the office of primate universally accepted in the western Church.[6] In later centuries the idea became mainly the subject of mere local controversy.[7]

The primacy contest involved more than the use of a title or the mere assertion of precedence. The essential problem for any claimant was to have his claim recognised. This always involved an outside power – in Ireland after the invasion either the royal government or the papacy. By the end of the eleventh century, the bishop of Dublin had built up an apparently impregnable and permanent leadership over the infant hierarchy. Not only was his diocese the first to be established in the reform, but it had been founded with papal authority and given quasi-legatine status symbolised in the sending of apostolic relics. As other dioceses were being formed, the bishop of Dublin was the active leader and guide in the early drive towards conformity with general Church practice. Lanfranc – himself interested in primatial ambitions in Britain – had recognised the bishop of Dublin as *pastor Hiberniae insulae metropolis*.[8] The O'Brian high-kings, Toirdealbach and Muirchertach, worked in close cooperation with both the bishop of Dublin and the archbishop of Canterbury to spread the ideas of reform in Ireland during the eleventh century. It was during the rulership of the former that the hereditary 'successor of Patrick', then a layman, had submitted himself and the traditional symbol of ecclesiastical hegemony, the *Bachal Iosa*, to the high-king in Dublin.[9] At the end of the century we find the bishop of Dublin emphasising his overall authority in the hierarchy by using the paraphenalia of an archbishop.[10] Then, at the beginning of the twelfth century, the first move was made to bring Armagh into the new diocesan system. Immediately thereafter Dublin's leadership in the hierarchy is challenged.

Despite skirmishes between the contestants, the primacy contest between Armagh and Dublin did not become a major preoccupation during most of the twelfth century. There are a number of reasons for this. It took most of the century before bishops in Armagh effectively seized ecclesiastical control from their predecessors, the hereditary lay 'successors of Patrick'. Secondly, resident papal legates were widely used during this century to accelerate the reform and their superior authority effectively quelled the ambitions of the contestants. A bishop centred somewhere in Meath was papal legate at the synod of Cashel in 1101. Gilbert the bishop of Limerick was legate at the synod of Raith Breasail in 1111. It was as bishop of Down that St Malachy was legate a few decades later. From 1148 the Cistercian bishop of Lismore was resident papal legate, and it was with him that Henry II dealt when arranging the council of Cashel in 1172. It was not until 1179 that Laurence O'Toole succeeded in joining the powers of legate and archbishop of Dublin.[11]

In 1106 the hereditary *comarba* at Armagh was induced to accept episcopal Orders. In joining the reform he brought with him the northern notions of hegemony.[12] The first evidence of this occurs five years later when the bishopric of Dublin was omitted from the first official ecclesiastical division of the country into dioceses which was drawn up in 1111.[13] Ten years later the reason for this omission is indicated.

Much has been written about the 'taking of the bishopric of Dublin' by the *comarba*-bishop of Armagh during the vacancy in Dublin of 1121. The suggestion that, as leader of the Irish hierarchy, the *comarba* of Armagh was bent on breaking the connection with Canterbury for the purpose of establishing a nationally independent hierarchy is unlikely. It hardly takes into account the fact that the principal participants in the synod of Raith Breasail ten years earlier, such as the high-king and the bishops of Limerick and Waterford, were working in the closest cooperation with the archbishop of Canterbury. There is also the fact that the candidate elected to the see of Dublin in 1121 was endorsed by the high-king, who wrote to England on his behalf to strengthen the request for consecration.[14] Besides, whatever 'taking the bishopric of Dublin' meant in 1121, Cellach the *comarba*-bishop of Armagh relinquished whatever he had 'taken' shortly afterwards, and the Canterbury-consecrated bishop of Dublin returned unmolested to his see. The Annals suggest an internal dispute in Dublin: 'Cellach, the *comarba* of Patrick, took the bishopric of Dublin by choice of the Foreigner and the Gael.'[15] A letter from the 'burgesses and entire clergy in the city of Dublin' to the archbishop of Canterbury tells another story: 'Know in truth that the bishops of Ireland have great envy against us, and especially that bishop who dwells in Armagh: because we are unwilling to obey their rules, but wish always to be under your government.'[16] Thus expressed, this desire is a new thing. During the eleventh century there was the closest collaboration between the leading bishops in Dublin on the one hand and the high-king and new bishops as they came into existence on the other. The new element which caused the special appeal to Canterbury was the battle for hegemony in the Church in Ireland. The Dubliners, bereft of a pastor, and of a leader to defend the prestige and status of the see, banked on the ambition of Canterbury to get them over the crisis. Their resistance was successful and bishop Gregory returned to Dublin. But the events of these years meant that the contestants in the new struggle for hegemony had emerged.

The vigorous Cellach of Armagh died in 1129. Thereafter the internal confusion in northern ecclesiastical circles effectively stultified any active campaign for leadership in the new hierarchy by the *comarbai* or bishops of Armagh. After years of difficulty, the bishop of Connor, Malachy O Morgair, gained some recognition as bishop of Armagh, but he relinquished this position shortly afterwards, appointed another to succeed him, and took over the bishopric of Down and made himself abbot of Bangor. By this time the hard-working Malachy had become the leader of the whole reform movement. His biographer tells of his consciousness that no metropolitan bishops had as yet been officially established in the country.[17] In 1139 or 1140 he set out for Rome to seek the necessary *pallia*. Pope Innocent II promised eventual papal endorsement for the establishment of metropolitans, but he bade Malachy return home – as papal legate – and have a solemn request made to Rome in the name of all the bishops and chieftains. His biographer implies that it was Malachy's intention to establish metropolitan bishops in Armagh and Cashel, but as the events demonstrate the papal curia was more fully aware of Irish conditions than the bishop of Down had imagined. It took eight more years to hold a meeting of all concerned to make the formal request for the *pallia*. The fact that the meeting was held on an island off Skerries in Dublin is possibly significant.[18] The outcome of this synod of 1148 was the coming of Cardinal John Paparo in 1152 and the establishment of the four metropolitan sees, in Armagh, Cashel, Dublin and Tuam. Although we have no contemporary documents, it is possible that the *primas totius Hiberniae* was applied to the archbishop of Armagh at the council of 1152 which the cardinal legate convened at Keils.[19] From this date onwards, the archbishop of Armagh is often referred to in contemporary documents, both Latin and Irish, as 'primate of all-Ireland'.

It has been asserted that the geographical notion of 'all-Ireland' was adopted in imitation of British usage. It may well have been, since there were two major contestants for the primacy in that land also, but the title 'all-Ireland' was used in Irish sources long before 1152. The battle for political hegemony produced a king of 'all-Ireland' as early as 861.[20] A *comarba* who was *apostolicus doctor totius Hiberniae* appears in 928.[21] We find the title 'all-Ireland' used in native sources to refer to legates, e.g. 'Laurence, archbishop of Dublin and legate of all-Ireland died' is an entry for the year 1180.[22] It is fairly clear that the use of the two titles in the primacy controversy, 'Ireland' and 'all-Ireland' was adopted from earlier usage, and that these titles were not invented specifically to designate the contestants for ecclesiastical hegemony in the twelfth century.

If a primatial title is sometimes used by the archbishop of Armagh after 1152, it is clear that this usage did not always correspond with a position of real power or precedence. In 1161, Laurence O'Toole became archbishop of Dublin, and he found himself, for a variety of reasons, the acknowledged leader of both the hierarchy and the Irish kings. For a time he was papal legate; he represented his country in the delicate negotiations with the English king; he held the council at Clonfert in 1179 in accordance with the instructions of the Third Lateran Council, and, returning Cellach's compliment of 1121, he appointed a western bishop as archbishop of Armagh in 1180. Until after the turn of the century no attempt was made from Armagh to challenge the hegemony of Dublin or assert an effective primacy over the Church in Ireland. The greatest problem for the incumbents at Armagh in these years was to establish themselves in their own territory, because the still-entrenched hereditary ecclesiastical chieftains continued to challenge their status. Meantime, the status and prestige which Laurence had reaffirmed for the see of Dublin was immediately adopted by his two powerful Norman successors. John Comyn was an active reformer who held the provincial council of Dublin in 1186, but he was also a shrewd politician. He sought and obtained papal confirmation for the independence of the province of Dublin from any pretensions by others.[23] His successor, Henry of London, a far less amiable customer, had himself made papal legate for Ireland and royal governor simultaneously. With the *de facto* recognition of both authorities, he formally canonised the status and prestige of the see of Dublin into a primacy early in the thirteenth century. The title on his episcopal seal was 'primate of Ireland'.[24]

The first sign that the archbishop of Armagh would put his own pretentions to primacy to a test came in 1215-16. At the General Council of the Lateran, the archbishop of Tuam complained to the Pope that the archbishop of Armagh had unlawfully despoiled him of two western bishoprics and a number of individual churches in the province of Connacht. Thinking in terms of continental bishoprics, the Pope was clearly baffled by the arguments put forward by the northern archbishop, since he admitted that the churches in question were located in an entirely different province. Subsequently it appears that the archbishop of Armagh was referring to the ancient customary rights of his hereditary predecessors over the 'churches of Patrick' in Connacht. The papal decision was given in favour of the archbishop of Tuam whose episcopal rights were not to be challenged.[25] The contest between the two archbishops for metropolitan rights over the diocese of Ardagh continued for some decades. The matter came up before Pope Gregory IX in 1235.[26] Then in 1241 the Annals tell us, peace was made between the two metropolitans concerning 'Patrick's land in Connacht'. But in the same year, the Annals also tell us, the newly appointed German archbishop of Armagh, Albert Suerbeer, arrived in Ireland with a bull of Pope Gregory IX granting him privileges over 'the churches of Patrick'.[27]

The advent of this largely absentee German ecclesiastic brought a new element into the Armagh pretensions to primatial status. For the first time the northern claim would be expressed in Pseudo-Isidorian terms. We find the archbishops of Cashel and Dublin, with their suffragans, joining together to issue a statement. Under no circumstances will they tolerate the expansion of primatial claims to their provinces.[28] A close look at the situation in Ireland seems to have convinced Albert Suerbeer that he had no hope of asserting primatial claims or rights over the province of Dublin. Against Cashel and Tuam he decided to try his luck. In 1244 we find Pope Innocent IV setting up a commission to investigate the claims of the archbishop of Armagh to primatial jurisdiction over the provinces of Cashel and Tuam, claims which, the Pope notes, were being vigorously resisted by the metropolitans of the south and west.[29]

Thereafter, the primacy controversy became mostly a paper war between the archbishops of Armagh and Dublin, and it was almost entirely confined to the self-interest of the prelates. Since the significance of the title depended in large measure on recognition by either the Popes or the government, the dispute remained fairly muted before the Reformation. After the Reformation both churches retained their two sets of primates. For the Anglican Church the issue was always held in check by the government, but because the Popes and the royal government were now divorced, the issue in the Catholic Church often took on ridiculous proportions. It was against this extraordinary vehemence, almost bitterness, that had crept into the primacy dispute that Archbishop Talbot of Dublin was reacting in 1670.

References

Chapter 1

1 The best general account of the Norman invasion is still Edmund Curtis, *A History of Medieval Ireland from 1086 to 1513* (London 1923, 1938). An indispensable corrective to this is J. F. Lydon, *The Lordship of Ireland in the Middle Ages* (Dublin 1972) which incorporates much recent investigation, especially of an economic and commercial nature.

2 Kenney, J., *The Sources for the Early History of Ireland* (New York 1929), 758.

3 See Sheehy, M. P., 'The Bull *Laudabiliter*: A Problem in Medieval Diplomatique and History', *Journal of the Galway Archaeological and Historical Society* XXIX nos. iii & iv (1961), 57-58.

4 *Metalogicon*, ed. Webb, C. C. (Oxford 1919) IV, 42.

5 O'Doherty, J. F., 'St Laurence O'Toole and the Anglo-Norman Invasion', *IER* L (1937), 459.

6 On John of Salisbury's manipulation of evidence, see Maccarrone, M. *Papato e Impero dalla elexione di Frederico I alla morte di Adriano IV* (Rome 1959), 77 n. 76.

7 For a full discussion of the *Laudabiliter* question, see Sheehy, *loc. cit.* and Watt, J., *The Church and the Two Nations in Medieval Ireland* (Cambridge 1970), 35ff.

8 Latin text in Sheehy, M. P., *Pontificia Hibernica: Medieval Papal Chancery Documents concerning Ireland. 640-1261* (Dublin 1962), no. 4.

9 Curtis, *op. cit.*, 49-50.

10 *Ibid.*, 52.

11 O'Doherty, *loc. cit.*, 468.

12 *Ibid.*

13 *Expugnatio Hibernica*, ed. Dimock, J. F. *Giraldi Cambrensis Opera V* (London 1867), 258.

14 O'Doherty, *loc. cit.*, 470.

15 *Expugnatio Hibernica*, 283.

16 Latin texts in Sheehy, *Pontificia Hibernica*, nos. 5-7.

17 *Eriu* VII (1914), 244.

18 *The first version of The Topography of Ireland by Giraldus Cambrensis* trans. by O'Meara, J. (Dundalk 1951), *passim.*

CHAPTER 2

1 See especially Lydon, *op. cit.*

2 See Lydon, J. F., 'The Problem of the Frontier in Medieval Ireland', *Topic* 13 (1967), 5ff.

3 *Irish Historical Documents, 1172-1922*, ed. Curtis & McDowell (London 1943), 22-3.

4 *Annals of Tighernach*, ed. Stokes, W. *Revue Celtique XVIII* (1897), 293.

5 *Expugnatio Hibernica*, 388ff.

6 O'Connor, F., *The Backward Look* (London 1967), 85.

CHAPTER 3

1 *De Rebus a se gestis II, xiii-xv Giraldi Cambrensis Opera I* ed. Brewer, J. S. (London 1861), 65ff.

2 Sheehy, *Pontificia Hibernica*, no. 22.

3 *Ibid.*, nos. 52, 144.

4 *Ibid.*, nos. 87-91.

5 *Ibid.*, no. 109.

6 *Ibid.*, nos. 139-140.

7 *Ibid.*, no. 141.

8 *Ibid.*, no. 144.

9 *Ibid.*, no. 158.

10 *Calendar of Documents relating to Ireland* 1171-1251, no. 1081.

11 *Ibid.*, no. 1840.

12 *Ibid.*, no. 1443.

13 Text in *Pontificia Hibernica* II, no. 440 n.1.

CHAPTER 4

1 *Expugnatio Hibernica*, 359.

2 See MacNiocaill, G., 'The Charters of John Lord of Ireland to the See of Dublin'. *Reportorium Novum* III no 2 (1963-1964), 285. Of the approximately 150 extant charters of Prince John, granted between 1185 and 1199 when he became king, nearly a third were grants to the new Church.

3 *De Rebus a se gestis*, 65, 87.

4 Latin text Sheehy, *Pontificia Hibernica*, no. 16.

5 Latin text *The Dignitas Decani of St Patrick's Cathedral Dublin*, ed. White, N. (Dublin 1957), 1.

6 See *Medieval Religious Houses in Ireland* by Gwynn & Hadcock (London 1969).

7 *Registrum Epistolarum Stephani de Lexinton*, ed. Griesser; Bruno, P., *Analecta Ordinis Cisterciensis* II (1946) *passim*; and Watt, J., *The Church and the Two*

Nations, chapter 4, 'The Crisis of the Cistercian Order', 85ff.

8 Sheehy, *Pontificia Hibernica*, nos. 34-35, 40-41 and notes.

9 *Ibid.*, nos. 34, 55, 62.

10 *Ibid.*, no 33. See also Dunning, P. J., 'Pope Innocent III and the Ross Election Controversy, 1198-1216', *ITQ* XXVI (1959), 346ff.

11 *Ibid.*, no. 52 and notes. See also Watt *op. cit.*, 226ff.

12 *Calendar of Documents relating to Ireland*, no. 291.

13 *Ibid.*, no. 346.

14 *Ibid.*, no. 512-13.

15 Documents in Sheehy, *Pontificia Hibernica*, nos. 57-58, 73, 128, 132. See also Dunning, P. J., 'Pope Innocent III and the Waterford-Lismore Controversy', *ITQ* XXVIII (1961), 215ff.

16 *Documents relating to Ireland* no. 168.

17 See Gwynn, A., 'Henry of London, Archbishop of Dublin', *Studies* XXXVIII (1949), 295-306, 389-402.

18 Gwynn, *loc. cit.*

19 See Dunning, 'Irish Representatives and Irish Ecclesiastical Affairs at the Fourth Lateran Council', *Medieval Studies presented to Aubrey Gwynn* (Dublin 1961), 90.

20 Gwynn, *loc. cit.*, 297.

21 Documents in *Pontificia Hibernica*, nos. 87-91, 93-97, 99, 100, 102-04, 106, 108.

22 Quoted in Gwynn, *loc. cit.*, 303.

23 *Ibid.*

24 See Hand, G., 'The Medieval Chapter of St Patrick's Cathedral, Dublin', *Reportorium Novum* III, no 2 (1963-64), 229-48.

25 *Calendar of Archbishop Alen's Register*, ed. McNeill, C. (Dublin 1950), 44.

26 *Pontificia Hibernica*, nos. 111-13, 126-27, 165-66, 171, 178-79.

27 Gwynn, *loc. cit.*, 389.

28 *Pontificia Hibernica*, nos. 135-37.

29 *Ibid.*, nos. 139, 140-41, 144, 158, 165-66.

30 *Annals of Loch Ce*, ed. Hennessy, W. M. (London 1871), 263.

31 *Medieval Irish Lyrics*, trans. James Carney (Dublin 1967), 81.

CHAPTER 5

1 Sheehy, *Pontificia Hibernica*, no. 88.

2 Hughes, K., *The Church in Early Irish Society* (London 1966), 272-73.

3 See MacNiocaill, G., *Notitiae as Leabhar Cheanannais*, 1033-1161 (Dublin 1961) and other twelfth century charters printed in Dugdale *Monasticon Anglicanum* II (London 1661).

4 See Binchy, D., *Studies in Early Irish Law* (Dublin 1935), 207-234.

5 Hughes, *loc. cit.*, 274.

6 *Pontificia Hibernica*, no. 235.

7 *Calendar of Documents relating to Ireland*, 1285-1292 (London 1879), 9-10.

8 Bieler, L., 'Insular Palaeography', *Scriptorium* III (1949), 283.

9 See Binchy, D., 'The Passing of the Old Order', *Proceedings of the International Congress of Celtic Studies* (Dublin 1962), 129.

10 See Meyer, K., *Ancient Irish Poetry* (Dublin 1962), 113.

11 O'Connor, F., *The Backward Look*, 87.

12 Giollabhrighde Mac Conmidhe in *Kings, Lords and Commons* (London 1961), 78.

13 O'Connor, *The Backward Look*, 91.

14 *Ibid.*, 89-90.

15 *Ibid.*, 91.

16 See *Pontificia Hibernica* II (Dublin 1965) no 307, n.1.

17 *Annals of Ulster*, ed. McCarthy, B. II (Dublin 1893), 133.

18 *Ibid.*,139-141.

19 *Expugnatio Hibernica*, 281-83.

20 *Annals of Tighernach*, *loc. cit.*, 286.

21 See the Irish comment on this legate's activities, above chapter 1, n. 17.

22 A detailed treatment of this controversy in Watt, *op. cit.*, 226ff.

23 *Annals of Clonmacnoise*, ed. Murphy, D. (Dublin 1896) 213. See also Gwynn, 'St Laurence O'Toole as Legate in Ireland', *Analecta Bollandiana* LXVIII(1950), 223ff.

24 *Pontificia Hibernica*, no. 21.

25 *Ibid.*, no. 53.

26 See Gwynn, 'Armagh and Louth', *Seanchas Ardmhacha* I (1954) 1-11; II (1955) 17.

27 *Pontificia Hibernica*, II nos. 292, 457 and nn.

28 *Ibid.*, no. 39.

29 *Ibid.*, no. 50.

30 'Chronicle of Melrose', in Anderson, *Early Sources of Scottish History*, II (Edinburgh 1722), 357.

31 *Annals of the Four Masters*, ed. O'Donovan, J., I (Dublin 1848), 127.

32 *Annals of Ulster*, II, 239.

33 *Annals of Loch Ce*, I, 315.

34 *Pontificia Hibernica*, II nos. 67n, 266, 289, 328n.

35 *Ibid.*, no. 53.

36 *Ibid.*, nos. 110, 240.

37 *Annals of Clonmacnoise*, 224.

38 *Pontificia Hibernica*, no. 100.

39 *Annals of Loch Ce*, I, 353-57. For further developments in this controversy, see Watt, *op. cit.*, 113.

40 *Calendar of Documents relating to Ireland*, 1171-1251, no. 481.

41 *Annals of Loch Ce*, I, 255.

42 *Calendar of Archbishop Alen's Register*, 40.

43 *Pontificia Hibernica*, nos. 38, 47-49.

44 *Annals of Ulster*, II, 239-40.

45 *Ibid.*, 257.

46 *Ibid.*, 265-67.

47 *Ibid.*, 245-47.

48 *Annals of Clonmacnoise*, 220.

49 *Medieval Irish Lyrics*, ed. Carney, J., 93.

50 *Pontificia Hibernica*, no. 141.

51 *Ibid.*, nos. 140, 158.

52 *Ibid.*, no. 138.

53 *Annals of Loch Ce*, I, 265, 271.

54 See Murphy, G., 'Eleventh and Twelfth Century Irish Doctrine concerning the Real Presence', *Medieval Studies presented to Aubrey Gwynn*, 19ff.

55 *Annals of Loch Ce*, I, 269.

CHAPTER 6
1 Watt, *op. cit.*, 215.

APPENDIX I
4a Source: See Falkenstein's study *loc. cit.*, 107-159.
1 Possibly Donnchadh Ua Cearbhaill, king of Oirghialla, but see Falkenstein, *loc. cit.*, 127ff.
2 *Ibid.*, 131ff.

APPENDIX II
1 *Primatus Dubliniensis vel summa rationum quibus innitur ecclesia Dubliniensis in possessione, ac prosecutione sui iuris ad Hiberniae Primatum* by Peter Talbot (Lille 1674), 1.
2 Hughes, K., *The Church in Early Irish Society*, 89-90.
3 Binchy, D., 'Patrick and his Biographers, Ancient and Modern', *Studia Hibernica*, II (1962), 59-60, 61.
4 Hughes, *op. cit.*, 111ff.
5 Kenney, *Sources for the Early History of Ireland*, 353-54.
6 Fuhrmann, H., 'Studien zur Geschichte mittelälterlicher Patriarchate', *Zeitschrift der Savigny-Stiftung für Rechtsgeschichte, Kan. Abt.* LXX (1953) 112ff., LXXI (1954) 1ff., LXXII (1955) 95ff.
7 In the seventeenth century controversy between Oliver Plunkett of Armagh and Peter Talbot of Dublin, they both appealed to the Pseudo-Isidorian Decretals.
8 *The Whole Works of the Most Rev. James Ussher*, IV (Dublin 1631), 488.

9 *Annals of Ulster, Annals of Inisfallen, Annals of Loch Ce*: all record this event.

10 Ussher, *Whole Works*, IV, 528-530. See also Gwynn, 'The First Bishops of Dublin', *Reportorium Novum*, I no. 1 (1955), 17ff.

11 See Gwynn, 'Papal Legates in Ireland in the 12th Century'. *IER* LXIII (1944) 361ff.

12 *Annals of Ulster*, II, 78.

13 See MacErlean, J., 'The Synod of Rath Breasail', *Archivium Hibernicum* III (1914), 1-33.

14 Ussher, *Whole Works*, IV, 534.

15 *Annals of Ulster*, II, 107.

16 Ussher, *loc. cit.*, 532.

17 *St Bernard of Clairvaux's Life of St Malachy of Armagh*, ed. Lawlor, H. J. (London 1920), 65.

18 *Ibid.*, 118; *Annals of the Four Masters*, II, 1083.

19 No contemporary records of the council of Kells of 1152 survive. Three lists of Irish bishops in Roman sources from about this date – lists which must have originated in the council of 1152 – use the title *primus totius Hiberniae* for the archbishop of Armagh, and no extra title for the archbishop of Dublin; see *Le Liber Censuum de l'Eglise Romaine*, ed. Duchesne (Paris 1901) I, 232, II, 101-02, and Lawlor, 'A Fresh Authority for the Synod of Kells', *PRIA* XXXVI, C (Dublin 1922), 17.

20 *Annals of Ulster*, I, 373.

21 *Annals of Ulster*, I, 451.

22 *Annals of Boyle*, ed. D'Alton (Dublin 1845), II, 304.

23 *Pontificia Hibernica*, nos. 11, 13, 14.

24 *Ibid.*, no. 148 and note 1. See also Watt, *op. cit.*, 109-12.

25 *Ibid.*, no. 100.

26 *Ibid.*, no. 220.

27 *Annals of Loch Ce*, 353-56.

28 *Crede Mihi: The Most Ancient Register Book of the Archbishops of Dublin before the Reformation*, ed. Gilbert (Dublin 1897), 60-61.

29 *Pontificia Hibernica*, no. 255. For further details see Watt, *op. cit.*, 112ff.

Brother Against Brother

Liam Deasy

Brother Against Brother is Liam Deasy's moving and sensitive account of the Civil War, Ireland's greatest tragedy. He recounts in detail the Republican disillusionment with the Truce and later with the Treaty, how the Republicans were hopelessly outnumbered, hunted and killed, especially in Munster, before they were finally broken and defeated. For the first time, Deasy recalls the circumstances surrounding his much-criticised order appealing to his comrades to call off the Civil War – an order that saved the lives of hundreds of prisoners.

Liam Deasy was born near Bandon in County Cork in 1896. He joined the Irish Volunteers in 1917 and on the formation of the West Cork Brigade of the IRA was appointed adjutant. He later became Brigade Commander. He took the Republican side in the Civil War and after it ended returned to civilian life, setting up a successful weatherproofing business. His celebrated account of the War of Independence, *Towards Ireland Free*, was published in 1973. He died in August 1974, while still working on *Brother Against Brother*.

MERCIER PRESS

HARRY BOLAND: A BIOGRAPHY

JIM MAHER

This is the first modern biography of a man who has been best known as a comrade and confidant – as well as rival in love – of Michael Collins.

As a member of the Irish Republican Brotherhood (IRB), Boland took part in the 1916 Rising and after his release from prison was appointed secretary to Sinn Féin. He played a prominent role in demanding political status for Irish prisoners in Britain. With Michael Collins he helped to build up the IRB and the Volunteers and organised the escape of Éamon de Valera from Lincoln Prison.

This volume gives a more comprehensive review of the six months prior to the Civl War (January to June 1922) than any previous publication. Boland's tragic death in the early days of the Civil War has gone down in popular history but this is the first time that the story of his last years and months has been fully told.

Jim Maher has spent many years researching the Civil War. He is also the author of a book on the War of Independence, *The Flying Columns – West Kilkenny*.

MERCIER PRESS

A Short History of Ireland

Sean McMahon

This short history of Ireland has already established itself as a classic and a bestseller. A concise and even-handed account, it gives the history of Ireland since the earliest times. Based upon up-to-date research, the book covers all political, social and cultural issues of importance. The author is particularly enlightening about the root causes of the Northern Troubles and the relationship between Britain and Ireland.

MERCIER PRESS